START SMART
MONEY BASICS

10 Money Principles
Every Young Adult Should Know

KAY • HAWLEY

Edited by Connie Anderson, Words & Deeds, Inc.

Book Cover and Interior Layout by Melissa Williams Design

Illustrations by Kay Hawley

Published by Northwoods Life Publishing

First Edition

ISBN: 979-8-9948888-0-3 (paperback)
ISBN: 979-8-9948888-1-0 (hardcover)
ISBN: 979-8-9948888-2-7 (eBook)

Disclaimer: This book provides general financial education and is not intended as personal financial, tax, legal, or investment advice. Readers should consult qualified professionals before making major financial decisions. The author and publisher assume no responsibility for actions taken based on the material presented.

Contact: www.kayhawley.com

For every young adult who was never taught this,
and is ready to begin anyway.

Contents

A Note Before You Begin vii
How to Use This Book viii

PART 1
Where Are You Now? *Self-Assessment* 1

Chapter 1: Seeing What Others Can't 1
Interlude: The Quiet Student 3
Chapter 2: The Balance in Life 4
Workbook: Your Ferris Wheel Assessment 9
Chapter 3: Where Are You Starting From? 18
Workbook: Start With Honesty—Your Money Right Now 24
Chapter 4: The Stories We Tell Ourselves 27
Workbook: Limiting Beliefs 34
Chapter 5: Your CAM Check-In 43
Workbook: Your CAM Check-In 47
Chapter 6: The 10 Money Realities 53
Workbook: The Money Reality Check 56

PART 2
Where Are You Going? *Vision and Goals* 59

Chapter 7: Meet Your Guides: The Start Smart Crew 61
Chapter 8: Clear the Path: Make the Right Choice the Easy Choice 65
Workbook: Clear the Path 72
Chapter 9: Define Your Freedom: What Are You Aiming for Right Now? 73
Workbook: Define Your Freedom 76
Chapter 10: Goals That Pull You Forward—Turning Vision Into Direction 79
Workbook: Goals That Pull You Forward 83

PART 3
How Will You Get There? *The 10 Principles* 85

Principle 1: Start Now, Even If It's Small 89
Principle 2: Pay Yourself First 92
Principle 3: Let Time and Consistency Do the Heavy Lifting 95

Principle 4: Build Your Safety Cushion ... **98**
Principle 5: Protect What Matters Most ... **101**
Principle 6: Keep More of What You Earn ... **105**
Principle 7: Keep It Simple, and Know Who Gets Paid ... **109**
Principle 8: Invest Intelligently with Help You Trust ... **113**
Principle 9: Teach It Forward ... **117**
Principle 10: Keep a Winning Attitude ... **120**
Interlude: Every Dollar You Earn Follows a Path ... *123*

PART 4
Real-Life Money Toolkit *Practical Tools* *125*

Start Here
Section 1: Money Mistakes You Don't Have to Make ... 127
Section 2: The Math That Actually Clicks ... 131
Section 3: Scripts for When the Pressure Is On ... 134
Section 4: Quick-Reference Cheat Sheets ... 138

Tools for Right Now
TOOL 1: Banking Basics—Opening Your Accounts ... 144
TOOL 2: Understanding Your Paycheck ... 145
TOOL 3: Your First Big Purchase—Transportation ... 146
TOOL 4: Renting 101 ... 148
TOOL 5: Protecting Yourself—Scams and Fraud ... 152
TOOL 6: Credit Cards and Building Credit ... 156
TOOL 7: Student Loans: What You Need Before You Borrow ... 158
TOOL 8: Money Management Worksheets ... 160

Tools For What Comes Next
TOOL 9: Credit Scores and Credit Reports ... 164
TOOL 10: Insurance Basics ... 168
TOOL 11: Student Loans: Repayment, Options, and Long-Term Planning ... 173
TOOL 12: Career and Income Decisions ... 176
TOOL 13: Consumer Protection and Digital Money ... 180
TOOL 14: Taxes—What You Need to Know Before You File ... 185
TOOL 15: Investing Basics ... 188
TOOL 16: How to Make Better Financial Decisions ... 192

PART 5

My Start Smart Financial Plan *Pulling It All Together* *197*

CAM Retake: Your Check-In 199

Section 1: Where I Am Now 205

Section 2: My Money Story 207

Section 3: My Financial Picture 209

Section 4: My Goals and My Plan 211

Section 5: One Thing I'll Teach 213

Before You Close This Book 214
A Note from Kay 215
Start Smart Quick Start Checklist 216
Acknowledgments 219
About the Author 220
Connect With Kay 221
About the Start Smart Series 222

A Note Before You Begin

When I was your age, no one taught me about money. I had a college degree, a solid career, and a paycheck, and I was still struggling. I knew something had to change, but I didn't know where to start.

Then I started finding mentors who opened my eyes to a different way of thinking about life and money, people who believed that ordinary individuals could understand and manage their own finances, and that belief completely changed how I saw things.

They didn't all speak the same way. One pushed me to start before I felt ready. Another slowed me down and helped me see clearly. One held me to my goals; another reminded me that my values had to lead. Each of them shaped how I think today.

Over time, those voices stayed with me. I'd hear them while making decisions: courage when I hesitated, clarity when I felt overwhelmed, common sense when things got complicated, balance when life felt heavy.

I taught instrumental music for more than 35 years and in all that time, one thing I saw over and over was this: the kids who struggled most weren't struggling because they weren't smart. They were struggling because nobody had ever shown them how. Money works the same way. When people finally get to see it clearly, panic becomes understanding, confusion becomes confidence, and shame becomes a choice.

So as you read, you won't be doing it alone. Throughout these pages, you'll occasionally hear from a group I call the Start Smart Crew, voices inspired by the real mentors and teachers who shaped my own journey. They represent the kinds of guidance we all need at different moments.

You'll meet them more fully in Chapter 7, but for now, just know they're here to help you pause, notice, and decide with intention.

My hope is simple: that what you find here gives you the tools, the language, and the courage to make money decisions that serve the life you actually want, starting exactly where you are because that's always the only place anyone can begin.

Kay Hawley—Edina, Minnesota

How to Use This Book

This isn't a book about getting rich. It's a book about learning to think clearly about money so you can make thoughtful choices in real life.

You don't need to read it cover to cover, absorb everything at once, or change everything right now. Some chapters will feel immediately useful. Others may make more sense later. You're free to move around, pause, reread, or skip ahead. Take what you need now, and come back for the rest when the time is right.

The book moves in five parts.

Part 1 — Where Are You Now? *see page 1*

Takes an honest look at your life and your money. This is not meant to judge you, but to give you a clear starting point.

Part 2 — Where Are You Going? *see page 59*

Helps you define what financial freedom really looks like for you right now, not someday, and not in theory.

Part 3 — How Will You Get There? *see page 85*

The 10 Principles gives you the strategy. Each principle is a tool, not a rule. You'll learn why it matters, hear a real story and find one small action you can adapt to your life.

Part 4 — Real-Life Money Toolkit *see page 125*

Provides step-by-step guides for banking, paychecks, cars, renting, student loans, protecting yourself from scams, and practical worksheets you can use right away.

Part 5 — My Start Smart Financial Plan *see page 197*

Brings everything together. You'll revisit your CAM Check-In, reflect on what you've learned, build your personal financial plan, and identify one thing you'll teach someone else.

After each chapter, you'll find a workbook section with writing prompts and one small action step. What you write on these pages is for you only.

You don't need to master all of this at once. What matters is that you keep moving forward. If this ever feels overwhelming, put the book down and then come back to it later. You're doing fine.

BEFORE YOU TURN THE PAGE

Take a breath. You are not behind, and you are not failing.

You are at the beginning, and the beginning is exactly the right place to be.

Let's begin.

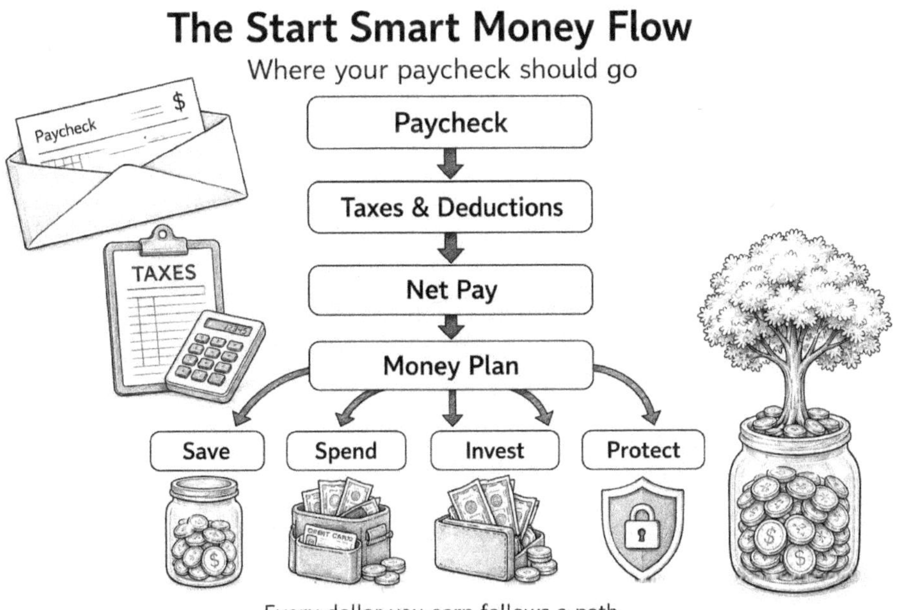

Every dollar you earn follows a path.
Smart money decisions start by understanding that path.

PART 1

Where Are You Now?

Self-Assessment

CHAPTER 1

Seeing What Others Can't

Perspective changes everything. I didn't learn that in a seminar. I learned it in a band room filled with seventh graders.

For much of my career, I taught junior high band. Every fall, a new group of students walked into my classroom, convinced they weren't ready, not fast enough, not musical enough, not good enough. Almost every year, before I could even take attendance, a hand would shoot up.

"Mrs. Hawley... are you going to tell us a story today?"

They knew me well. I loved telling stories because a good story could turn a restless classroom into a quiet one.

One of their favorites was about my brother, Jeff. He was a helicopter pilot in Vietnam in the early 1970s. He used to write home about the dangerous missions they flew. They would fly low above the treetops, going hundreds of miles an hour in the middle of the night. Can you imagine how dangerous that was?

The only way they could do that was by wearing night-vision goggles. Today we see these goggles in movies all the time, but back then most people had never even heard of anything like that.

Without those goggles, the mission would have been impossible. They gave my brother the ability to see clearly in complete darkness.

My students weren't dodging trees at midnight, though some days it came close. They were tackling complex music with limited experience and the quiet pressure to get it right, fast.

As they stepped into class, I'd fit each of them with an invisible pair of goggles, and with a snap of my fingers, turn them on. The glasses had two modes:

- **microscope** mode for tricky measures,

- and **telescope** mode for the sweep of the entire piece.

Zoom in. Zoom out.

Almost immediately, shoulders relaxed, panic eased, and eyes began moving differently across the page.

Sarah's fingers, which had been flying frantically across the keys, suddenly steadied. "Oh," she said quietly. "I see it now."

The music hadn't changed. *The way she looked at it had.*

Nothing was wrong with these students; they simply didn't know what to look for or how to practice.

Years later, when I began teaching financial awareness, I saw the same pattern. When Jessica told me she felt like a failure because she couldn't save money, we put on our microscope glasses. She saw it instantly: a $340 monthly car payment on a $28,000 salary, with student loans and rent taking half her paycheck. That was not failure; it was math.

Next, we switched to telescope mode. She would pay off the car in three years, then redirect every dollar of the payments toward savings. She was not stuck forever, but was in a temporary situation.

Most people assume something is wrong with them, though it usually is not. Nobody had handed them the glasses.

This book is about learning to see more clearly, not with perfect answers or strict rules, but by noticing patterns, asking better questions, and making thoughtful choices in everyday life. Money isn't just math. It shapes your stress, sleep, relationships, and freedom. When you learn to zoom in on what matters and zoom out to see where you're headed, you gain something more useful than a budget or a checklist, to gain perspective. Perspective gives you options.

The glasses are in your hands now. Put them on.

Interlude: The Quiet Student

Every music teacher knows this moment. There is always one student who sits quietly in the back of the ensemble. They play their part carefully, but they rarely stand out.

One spring concert, I decided to give a short solo to one of those quiet students. When I told her, her eyes got wide.

"Are you sure?" she asked.

She practiced that solo for weeks, slowly and carefully, over and over. The night of the concert arrived, and when the moment came, she stood up and played beautifully. When she finished, the audience erupted in applause.

Afterward, she said something I'll never forget: *"I didn't know I could do that."*

Sometimes confidence doesn't come before we try something new. Sometimes it comes because we try.

Money decisions can feel exactly the same way. Looking honestly at your spending for the first time, asking a question you were afraid sounded foolish, or taking one small step you weren't sure you were ready for, can all feel intimidating. Once you act, you often discover something that surprises you.

You realize you're more capable than you thought.

CHAPTER 2

The Balance in Life

Money is only one part of your life, but it touches almost everything else.

When I was in college, I was convinced that if I could just get the balance right, everything would fall into place. I taped a triangle to my mirror: mental, physical, spiritual. I studied it every morning. When that didn't work, I turned it into a ladder, adding rungs as I went: social, emotional, and eventually, financial. I kept rearranging the shape, convinced that one more category would finally do it. It never did.

No matter how hard I worked, something always felt off. When school went well, my health slipped. When I focused on relationships, work suffered. When I tried to hold everything together, I burned out. What I didn't yet understand was this: balance isn't a fixed point you reach. It's something you keep adjusting.

Before we talk about money, we're going to look at your whole life. Not because everything needs to be fixed before you can start, but because money doesn't exist in isolation. It connects to your sleep, your stress, your relationships, and your sense of possibility. When you can see those connections clearly, using telescope mode, you stop treating money as a separate math problem and start seeing it as part of the life you're really living.

The Ferris Wheel: Why Balance Matters More Than Perfection

Think of your life as a Ferris wheel. It keeps moving, whether you feel ready or not. Sometimes you're at the top, with a clear view of everything. Other times you're near the bottom, doing your best to simply get through the day. Those days count, too, because they're still part of the same ride.

Your life has eight connected cars:

- **Mental** — learning, focus, growth
- **Physical** — health, sleep, energy
- **Emotional** — stress, confidence, peace of mind
- **Social** — friends, connection, community
- **Spiritual** — values, purpose, what matters to you
- **Financial** — money, bills, savings, choices
- **Family** — your closest people
- **Work/School** — job, classes, career direction

These aren't random categories. Over decades of teaching, I saw that these were the areas that caused both the teacher and the students the most struggle when ignored for too long and also provided the most relief when given even a small amount of attention.

At any given moment, one seat on a Ferris wheel rides higher than all the others. On your Ferris wheel, that higher seat isn't better, it's simply where most of your time and energy are going right now. Something else sits lower, waiting for its turn. That's not failure. That's the wheel in motion. Your job isn't to keep every seat at the same level.

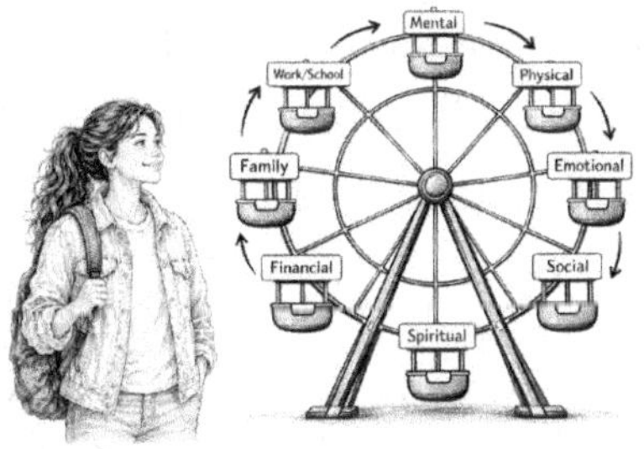

Your job is to **keep the wheel turning** so no area stays stuck at the bottom for too long.

What Balance Really Means for You

A lot of advice, especially financial advice, quietly assumes that the answer is simple: try harder, save more, spend less, and focus on the future. That advice assumes you have room to adjust, but many young people don't.

Some are working long shifts to stay afloat, with paychecks going almost entirely toward necessities. There isn't any extra money to redirect. There is only the next bill. Others don't have jobs yet and rely on parents, allowances, or gift money. They may feel uncertain about whether they should even think about money yet.

And then there are those of you who are doing both at once. You're in school full-time and working 20, 30, or sometimes 40 hours a week. You're running on too little sleep, eating whatever is fast and cheap, and trying to keep your grades up between shifts. Advice that works when you have time and energy affects you very differently when you're running on empty. I know that. This book is trying to meet you where you really are.

For some readers, money decisions involve the whole family, not only the individual. If you regularly send money home, contribute to household expenses, help support siblings, or care for a family member, that is a real financial responsibility, and this book accounts for it. You are not behind because your situation is more complex. You are working with a greater amount of responsibility than most.

When someone is told, "You should really save more," it doesn't always feel helpful. It can feel disconnected from reality. Forcing perfect balance during a hard season doesn't bring peace. It brings guilt.

Balance involves recognizing when you've neglected something for too long, allowing yourself to make changes, and establishing small, consistent habits that maintain momentum. There will be stretches when (1) school demands take the lead, (2) the family needs more of you, and (3) money must be the top priority. That is okay as long as **the wheel keeps turning.**

This book will spend extra time on your financial Ferris wheel car because money can either open doors or quietly close them. Money works best when it serves your whole life, not the other way around. *Your worth is not your bank balance.*

Two Lives, Same Pattern

Maya and Jordan are two of the Start Smart Crew you will see throughout this book. Their situations differ, but the thinking behind their choices matters.

Example 1: Maya—High School Junior (No Job, Parent-Supported)

Maya is 17, a high school junior without a job during the school year. Her money comes from a monthly allowance, birthday checks, and occasional gifts from relatives. She avoids tracking her spending because she's unsure she wants to know.

Over time:

- Money feels unpredictable → Financial drops
- Asking parents for money feels awkward → Emotional drops
- She avoids tracking spending → Mental drops

After her birthday, she realizes she does not know what happened to last year's gift money. She makes one small choice: any money she receives gets split into three simple buckets: spend now, save for later, and share or give. Doing this makes money feel less mysterious.

Example 2: Jordan—High School Senior (Working, Surviving)

Jordan is 19 and works long hours at a coffee shop. Over time, the constant work drains his focus. No time for friends leaves him isolated. Anxiety builds quietly until a small mistake at work makes him pause and take stock of what's happening.

- Over time with constant work → Mental drops
- No time for friends → Social drops
- Anxiety builds → Emotional drops

He realizes he has been reacting to his life instead of getting ahead of it. He makes a few adjustments: shorter shifts, simple meals, protected evenings. Nothing is perfect. He feels steadier and more grounded.

Two different starting points. Same lesson: small, consistent choices keep the wheel moving. That is all balance ever really is.

WORKBOOK: CHAPTER 2

YOUR FERRIS WHEEL ASSESSMENT

Part 1: Rate Your Ferris Wheel

Circle the number that best reflects how each area feels right now. This is about awareness, not accuracy.

1 = Very Low | 5 = Very Strong

Mental — Learning, Focus, Growth	1 · 2 · 3 · 4 · 5
Physical — Health, Sleep, Energy	1 · 2 · 3 · 4 · 5
Emotional — Stress, Confidence, Peace of Mind	1 · 2 · 3 · 4 · 5
Social — Friends, Connection, Community	1 · 2 · 3 · 4 · 5
Spiritual — Values, Purpose, What Matters	1 · 2 · 3 · 4 · 5
Financial — Money, Bills, Savings, Choices to You	1 · 2 · 3 · 4 · 5
Family — Your Closest People	1 · 2 · 3 · 4 · 5
Work / School — Job, Classes, Direction	1 · 2 · 3 · 4 · 5

Part 2: Notice Without Judging

Which area of your wheel feels highest right now?

____

____

Which feels lowest or most ignored?

Does anything surprise you?

Part 3: Inner Peace Check-In

Right now, how peaceful does your life feel overall? Circle one.

Very Unsettled — Somewhat Unsettled — Neutral

Mostly Calm — Grounded and Steady

What seems to disturb your peace most right now?

Part 4: Set Your Goals—One Area at a Time

For each area, write one short-term goal (next three to six months) and one long-term goal (about a year or longer). Keep it real and doable. Your first instinct is usually good enough.

See how Maya and Jordan filled this out, then write your own answers on the pages that follow.

EXAMPLE 1: Maya's Life in Motion
Maya—High School Junior

Mental: *Your intellect, learning, curiosity, and mental growth*

Short-Term Goal (next 3–6 months): Stop studying with my phone on the desk. One focused hour per subject before I check anything, especially my phone.

Long-Term Goal (1 year or more): Finish junior year with grades I truly earned, not ones I scrambled for the night before.

Physical: *Your health, energy, body, and movement*

Short-Term Goal (next 3–6 months): Get to bed before midnight on school nights at least four days a week.

Long-Term Goal (1 year or more): Have enough energy to get through the day without feeling exhausted by third period.

Emotional: *Your feelings, processing, and inner life*

Short-Term Goal (next 3–6 months): Stop pretending everything is fine when it isn't. Talk to one person I trust when things feel heavy.

Long-Term Goal (1 year or more): Feel less anxious about the future by focusing on what I can actually control right now.

Social: *Your relationships, community, and connections*

Short-Term Goal (next 3–6 months): Spend less time on my phone when I'm with friends and be present with them.

Long-Term Goal (1 year or more): Have a small group of people I can count on, not just a lot of people I sort of know.

Spiritual: *Your deeper purpose, values, and meaning*

Short-Term Goal (next 3–6 months): Figure out what I actually care about, not what my parents or friends think I should care about.

Long-Term Goal (1 year or more): Make at least one decision this year that is fully mine, based on my own values.

Financial: *Your resources, security, and freedom*

Short-Term Goal (next 3–6 months): Track every dollar I spend for one month, even small purchases like coffee or snacks.

Long-Term Goal (1 year or more): Save $200 from babysitting or odd jobs by the end of the school year so I have something to work with.

Family: *Your closest relationships, responsibilities, and love*

Short-Term Goal (next 3–6 months): Stop arguing about small things and pick my battles more carefully at home.

Long-Term Goal (1 year or more): Have a better relationship with my parents by being more honest with them about what I need.

Work/School: *Your career, contribution, and direction*

Short-Term Goal (next 3–6 months): Research two or three things I might in fact want to do after high school, with no pressure to decide yet.

Long-Term Goal (1 year or more): After graduation, have at least a general direction, even if the details aren't figured out.

EXAMPLE 2: Jordan's Life in Motion

Jordan—High School Senior

Mental: *Your intellect, learning, curiosity, and mental growth*

Short-Term Goal (next 3–6 months): Stay on top of deadlines for the next two months instead of waiting until the last minute.

Long-Term Goal (1 year or more): Graduate with grades that reflect what I'm capable of, not what I got away with.

Physical: *Your health, energy, body, and movement*

Short-Term Goal (next 3–6 months): Walk or move for at least 20 minutes a day, even on days when I don't feel like it.

Long-Term Goal (1 year or more): Build a routine now that doesn't completely fall apart when I move out and find a place of my own.

Emotional: *Your feelings, processing, and inner life*

Short-Term Goal (next 3–6 months): Write down what I'm stressed about instead of letting it build up until I snap.

Long-Term Goal (1 year or more): Go into whatever comes next after feeling ready, not just relieved the year is over.

Social: *Your relationships, community, and connections*

Short-Term Goal (next 3–6 months): Be intentional about which friendships I want to carry forward after graduation.

Long-Term Goal (1 year or more): Stay connected to the people who really matter, even when life gets busy and pulls us in different directions.

Spiritual: *Your deeper purpose, values, and meaning*

Short-Term Goal (next 3–6 months): Think about what kind of person I want to be, not only what I want to do for work.

Long-Term Goal (1 year or more): Make decisions that I can look back on and feel good about.

Financial: *Your resources, security, and freedom*

Short-Term Goal (next 3–6 months): Open a savings account and put at least $25 a month in it, even if it feels small.

Long-Term Goal (1 year or more): Have at least $500 saved so I'm not starting from zero.

Family: *Your closest relationships, responsibilities, and love*

Short-Term Goal (next 3–6 months): Have one honest conversation with my parents about what I'm thinking and feeling about next year after I graduate.

Long-Term Goal (1 year or more): Figure out how to be independent without losing the people who care about me most.

Work/School: *Your career, contribution, and direction*

Short-Term Goal (next 3–6 months): Apply to two or three realistic options after graduation, whether that's college, trade school, or a job.

Long-Term Goal (1 year or more): Have a clear next step, even if the whole plan isn't figured out yet.

| Your Turn: A Life in Motion |

Maya and Jordan have completely different goals. Yours will look different too. Write what is true for you right now, not what sounds good on paper.

Mental: *Your intellect, learning, curiosity, and mental growth*

Short-Term Goal (next 3–6 months):

____

____

Long-Term Goal (1 year or more):

____

____

Physical: *Your health, energy, body, and movement*

Short-Term Goal (next 3–6 months):

____

____

Long-Term Goal (1 year or more):

____

____

Emotional: *Your feelings, processing, and inner life*

Short-Term Goal (next 3–6 months):

____

____

Long-Term Goal (1 year or more):

____

____

Social: *Your relationships, community, and connections*

Short-Term Goal (next 3–6 months):

____

____

Long-Term Goal (1 year or more):

____

____

Spiritual: *Your deeper purpose, values, and meaning*

Short-Term Goal (next 3–6 months):

____

____

Long-Term Goal (1 year or more):

____

____

Financial: *Your resources, security, and freedom*

Short-Term Goal (next 3–6 months):

____

____

Long-Term Goal (1 year or more):

____

____

Family: *Your closest relationships, responsibilities, and love*

Short-Term Goal (next 3–6 months):

____

____

Long-Term Goal (1 year or more):

____

____

Work/School: *Your career, contribution, and direction*

Short-Term Goal (next 3–6 months):

____

____

Long-Term Goal (1 year or more):

____

____

Part 5: One Small Shift

You do not need to fix your whole wheel, but notice one thing.

Which one area feels heaviest right now?

____

What is one small, realistic choice you can make this week?

____

____

CHAPTER 3

Where Are You Starting From?

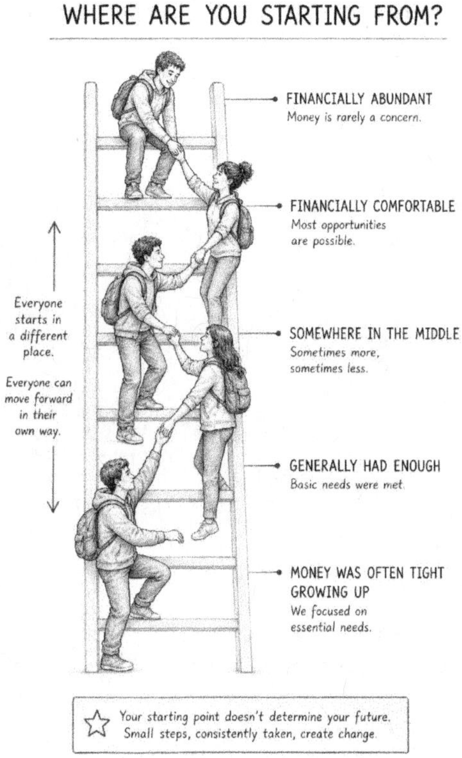

Everyone grows up with a different money story, and those stories vary widely. Some families have very little, others have plenty, and many fall somewhere in between. Understanding your starting point helps you see your situation more clearly, because there is no single right place to begin. What matters is learning to make thoughtful decisions from wherever you are.

You've already looked at your life using the Ferris wheel. Now we're going to zoom in on finances.

This isn't a book about getting rich. It's a book about getting free. That means different things to different people. For some, it means being able to say yes to dinner with friends without checking their balance first. For others, it means sleeping through the night without bills on their mind, or finally working at a job they chose rather than one they settled for. Whatever it looks like for you, the goal is the same: enough breathing room to make your own choices.

Money, used wisely, doesn't only buy things. It gives you more options.

Your life might look like many things right now. You might work part time while in school, barely covering expenses. You might start a full-time job but be weighed down by student loans. You may live at home, working multiple jobs to save for your independence, and still feel the pinch, or you might earn a nice income but watch your money disappear each month. You may send a portion of every paycheck home to family, which is a real and honorable financial responsibility, not a detour from good money management.

You are at the starting line, and that is exactly where this kind of work begins. The habits you build now will stick with you longer than you expect.

When money feels stressful, the questions we ask often sound like this:

- Why am I so bad with money?
- Why can't I ever get ahead?
- Why is everyone else doing better than I am?

Those questions rarely get you very far. Try these instead:

- What is one small action I can take today to improve my situation?
- What would my life look like if I felt more in control of my money?
- What is already working that I can build on?

Starting with a better question usually gets you a better result.

Starting Points

See if you can relate to any of the experiences of these Crew members.

Lucas (Financially Abundant): Money and opportunities were rarely a concern. Travel, activities, and support were always available.

Maya (Financially Comfortable): Activities, lessons, and occasional extras were usually possible without major stress.

Jordan (Somewhere in the Middle): Friends came from many different situations, some with more, some with less.

Riley (Generally Had Enough): The family usually had what was needed. Some extras required planning or careful budgeting.

Diego (Money Was Often Tight): The family focused mainly on covering basic needs. They knew how to stretch a dollar.

Everyone starts somewhere, but everyone can climb. Your starting point does not determine your future. What matters most is the choices you make and the habits you build moving forward.

Your Money Messages

What money messages did you hear growing up? These are the phrases and ideas about money that came from parents, grandparents, friends, or your community. They often stay with us longer than we realize.

Examples might sound like:

- "We can't afford that."
- "Save your money."
- "Money doesn't grow on trees."
- "Work hard and you'll be okay."
- "Rich people are just lucky."

Money messages don't come only from family. They also come from culture, community, and faith. Some cultures expect you to help parents or extended family financially as soon as you are able. In others, moving out quickly and becoming independent is the norm.

Some communities talk openly about money; others treat it as private or even impolite to discuss. Some faith traditions teach that giving comes before saving. Others emphasize avoiding debt above all else.

None of these approaches is right or wrong. They've shaped what "normal" has looked like for you so far.

Write one or two messages you remember:

From your family or caregivers:

____

____

From your culture, community, or faith tradition:

____

____

**You don't have to agree with these messages.
For now, it's enough to notice them.**

Question 1 — Right Now (The Microscope)

The first question is this: How do you feel about handling money right now?

Do not answer what you think you should feel. Not what other people might say but what's true for you today.

This question asks you to zoom in, microscope mode, on your present reality. To name the stress, the confusion, or even the hope you feel when you think about money.

When you can name how something feels, it becomes less overwhelming. The feeling doesn't disappear, but it stops being a vague, heavy pressure. It becomes specific. When something is specific, it's easier to deal with.

Your answer might sound completely different from anyone else's. That's fine. There are no right answers, only honest ones. The important thing isn't how you feel about money right now. The important thing is that you're willing to name it, to bring it into the open and look at it clearly.

Question 2 — Looking Ahead (The Telescope)

The second question is this: What would financial freedom actually look like for you?

This question asks you to zoom out, telescope mode, and imagine what enough might feel like. Not what financial experts say you should want, or what looks impressive to others, but what would feel like freedom to you.

Your version might look nothing like anyone else's, and that's okay. Your financial freedom is yours to define.

Maybe it means not living paycheck to paycheck. Maybe it means having enough saved to get through three months without income. Maybe it means being able to help your parents or send money home without stressing you. Maybe it means working at a job you love instead of a job that pays the bills. Any of those would be worth working toward.

Take a moment to picture a regular Tuesday in a life where you feel financially steady. What's different from today? How does your body feel? What is and isn't on your mind?

Write a few lines in your own words:

The Gap Between Here and There

Once you've thought about both questions, how money feels now and what freedom would look like, something important happens. You see the gap.

That gap doesn't mean you're behind.

Owen says: "The gap isn't a verdict. It's a map. Two simple points: where you are and where you're headed. That space is where this book comes in."

You don't need to close that gap today, but you need to see it clearly.

A Story of Seeing Clearly: Riley's Job That Looked Better on Paper

Riley didn't have a car in his freshman year of college. When an off-campus job paying $20 an hour opened up, it felt like a win. It paid more than the $15-an-hour jobs available on campus, and Riley assumed higher pay meant more money.

On paper, that was true. In real life, the math told a different story. Bus fares or ride-shares, extra time getting to work and back, and a schedule that clashed with classes were problems. After running the real numbers, the on-campus job came out nearly the same in terms of take-home pay, with less stress, eight hours of commute time saved each month, and a schedule that fit around classes.

Riley didn't take the higher-paying job. Riley took the smarter one, after doing the math the job posting didn't show. That's the microscope in action: zooming in on the real numbers instead of the ones that look impressive on the surface.

WORKBOOK: CHAPTER 3

START WITH HONESTY: YOUR MONEY STORY RIGHT NOW

Writing Exercise 1: Right Now (The Microscope)

Lin says: "Seeing clearly where you are right now is the most useful thing you can do. Everything else starts from there."

Set a timer for three to five minutes. Write continuously without stopping, even if you repeat yourself or write "I don't know what to say." No editing. No judging. Just honest words.

Your money story is yours alone. Your starting point might involve supporting family, sending money home, giving to your faith community, or simply covering your basic needs. Whatever is true for you, write it.

Start with: *Right now, money in my life feels like...*

____

____

____

____

____

____

Writing Exercise 2: Looking Ahead (The Telescope)

Set a timer for three to five minutes and write without stopping again. Don't worry about being practical yet, but be honest about what you truly want.

Start with: *For me, financial freedom looks like...*

One-Minute Reflection

Look at both responses. What do you notice about the difference between your current answer and your looking-ahead answer?

You don't need to solve anything yet, but you must notice the gap. That space between where you are and where you want to be is where this book comes in. Keep both writing exercises. You'll return to them in Part 2 when you define your vision for financial freedom.

CHAPTER 4

The Stories We Tell Ourselves: Limiting Beliefs About Money

You've named how money feels right now and what financial freedom might look like in the future. Now we're going to look at the stories you might be telling yourself about money, not to judge them or fix them yet, but simply to notice them.

When you understand the stories behind your money choices, your actions start to make more sense. You can see why you avoid certain conversations, why you hesitate to look at your account, or why you feel behind even when you're working hard. When you can see the story, you can decide whether to keep it.

What Limiting Beliefs Really Are

A limiting belief isn't a flaw. It's a story you believe about yourself, often formed during times of stress, struggle, or comparison.

These stories sound like:

- "I'm just bad with money."
- "People like me never get ahead."
- "I'll always be broke."
- "Everyone else has it figured out."

None of these thoughts mean something is wrong with you. They mean you've absorbed a narrative, sometimes one that was never true, and sometimes one that was true once but doesn't have to remain true.

The tricky part is this: limiting beliefs feel like facts, and your brain accepts them as reality without flagging them as stories. They're interpretations, though, and interpretations can be questioned.

How Limiting Beliefs Form

Beliefs change when new evidence appears.

Limiting beliefs about money don't appear out of nowhere. They grow from early messages about money, what your family said or didn't say, whether money felt abundant, scarce, or off-limits. They grow from early struggles: over-drafting your account for the first time, watching a parent stress about bills, or feeling behind your peers financially. They grow from comparison, what you see on social media, and the feeling that you should be further along. They also grow from outside realities: student debt, low wages, high costs, and being the first in your family to navigate certain systems.

A single painful moment can do it too. One student received a generous birthday gift and spent it quickly on clothes and other things she wanted in the moment. Weeks later, when the money was gone, regret set in. "I'm so bad with money," she told herself, and she carried that belief for a long time.

Sometimes it isn't one big moment. It's a single bad experience with someone you trusted. Another student, careful and hardworking, invested $300 in something that turned out to be a scam; he wasn't careless, but he was targeted by someone who knew exactly what they were doing. The mistake left him feeling foolish, and that feeling stuck.

Sometimes the belief builds so slowly you don't even see it coming. Buying fast food between shifts, coffee every morning, and snacks at work added up to several hundred dollars a month that another student never saw coming, and that slow leak kept him feeling broke no matter how many hours he worked.

Money beliefs can also be shaped by culture, community, and identity. In some families or cultures, talking about money is considered private or even rude, so questions go unasked and confusion builds quietly. In others, young people are expected to help support parents or extended family as soon as they're able, which can create both pressure and pride at the same time. Some communities view wealth with suspicion; others see it as proof of hard work and character. These patterns aren't right or wrong. They are what you learned it meant to be a good person around money.

These experiences are real, and so are the feelings that come with them. The story you built from those experiences might not be accurate anymore. Stories that outlive the moment that created them don't have to follow you forever.

A Story from the Band Room

One of the most talented flute players I ever taught could barely get through a solo without stopping.

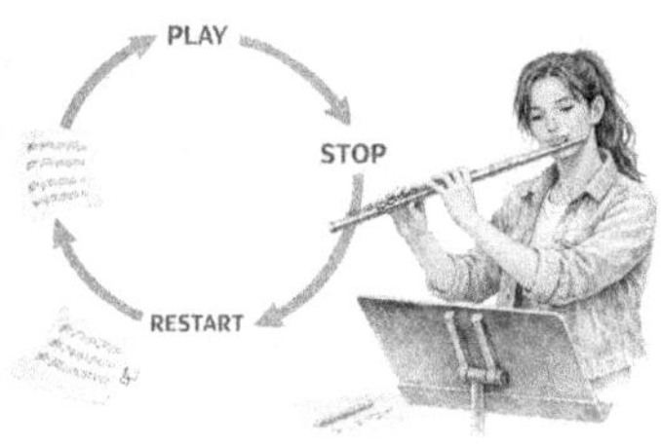

Without realizing it, she was practicing the pause instead of the music.

Every time she hit a difficult passage, she'd pause, shake her head, and start over. She'd done it so often that "I can't get through this" no longer felt like a thought. It felt like a fact. I pulled her aside after rehearsal. "You're not struggling with the music," I told her. "You're struggling with what you believe about the music."

We put on the microscope glasses and zoomed in on exactly four measures, the ones she always quit on. She played them slowly, then slower still, and by the end of one session she got through without stopping.

The notes were identical, but the belief behind them had shifted.

I've seen the same pattern in financial workshops. A person has been thinking, "I'm really bad with money," for so long that they flinch before even opening an app, and they become very good at not looking. The story was never true, but it was repeated so often that it started to feel true. What story have you been telling yourself about money?

Common Money Limiting Beliefs

→ Belief 1: "I'm Bad with Money"

What it sounds like: "I've always been bad with money. Numbers aren't my thing."

Why it feels true: You've made financial mistakes. You've overspent, avoided looking at your bank account, or felt confused by financial terms. Those moments feel like proof.

The reality: Being bad with money isn't a personality trait; it's a fixable knowledge gap. I've watched so many students prove this wrong in only one semester.

The reframe: "I'm learning about money" or "I haven't been taught this yet."

→ Belief 2: "I'll Never Get Ahead"

What it sounds like: "No matter what I do, I'm always broke. I'll never catch up."

Why it feels true: Progress feels slow, bills keep coming, and life keeps presenting emergencies. It's hard to see improvement when you're in survival mode.

The reality: "Never" is permanent language for temporary circumstances. What's true today doesn't have to be true in two years, if you make different choices with better information.

The reframe: "I haven't gotten ahead yet" or "Progress is slower than I'd like, but it's still progress."

→ Belief 3: "Everyone Else Has It Figured Out"

What it sounds like: "I'm the only one who doesn't know what I'm doing. Everyone else seems fine with money."

Why it feels true: You see what people show you, not what's actually happening.

The reality: Most people are working it out as they go. Many people who look financially secure are living paycheck to paycheck, carrying debt, or feeling stressed behind closed doors. You're not uniquely behind; you're being more honest about it.

The reframe: "Other people struggle too, even if I can't see it" or "I'm learning at my own pace."

→ Belief 4: "People Like Me Don't..."

What it sounds like: "People from my background don't build wealth. People in my family never get ahead."

Why it feels true: You may not have models of financial success in your immediate circle. If no one you know has done it, it can feel impossible.

The reality: Not seeing examples doesn't mean it's impossible. It means you might be among the first in your family or community to build financial security. That's hard, and it matters.

The reframe: "I might be the first in my family to build financial security, and that's okay" or "I'm writing a new chapter."

Why Limiting Beliefs Feel So Real

Limiting beliefs don't feel like opinions. They feel like facts. Once you believe something about yourself, your brain looks for evidence that supports it and ignores evidence that contradicts it.

A week with one overdraft fee feels bigger than three months of paying bills on time. That's how confirmation bias works, and it's not a personal failing. That's how the brain operates.

You also compare your messy reality to what other people choose to show you. You see their vacation photos, not their credit card debt. You see their new car, not their seven-year loan. You see their confident tone, not their private anxiety. That is not a fair comparison, and it was never meant to be one.

When you add in cultural and family expectations about what people like you are supposed to do with money, it can feel even more fixed. Expectations are not destiny. They're the starting script, and you're allowed to write a different one with your money than the one you grew up hearing.

Notice Without Judgment

You don't have to change your limiting beliefs today. Telling yourself to think positive or to believe differently rarely works, but paying attention does.

Notice the thoughts that arise when money makes you want to look away. When you avoid checking your bank account, what story is running? When anxiety kicks in, what do you actually believe?

These thoughts are like background music, always playing yet rarely noticed. When you start listening for them, you may be surprised by how often they show up. Once you can see those thoughts clearly, you can begin questioning them.

Questioning Your Beliefs (Gently)

When you've noticed a limiting belief, you can start questioning it, not with force or shame, but with curiosity.

- Is this actually true, or does it just feel true?
- What evidence contradicts this belief?
- Would I say this to a friend, or only to myself?
- What would I believe instead if I didn't believe this?

You're not trying to erase your history; you're testing whether the story you built from it still serves you.

Creating New Evidence

New beliefs grow from new evidence, and you create that evidence through what you do, especially the small things you repeat.

Old belief: "I'm bad with money."

Small action: Check your bank account three days in a row without panicking.

New evidence: "I can look at my money without avoiding it."

Updated belief: "I'm learning to face the truth about my money instead of avoiding it."

Taking small actions creates new evidence, and new evidence is what changes the story.

WORKBOOK: CHAPTER 4

LIMITING BELIEFS: NOTICING, QUESTIONING, AND REFRAMING

Part 1: Identify Your Limiting Beliefs

Take a minute to be honest with yourself here.

When money feels hard, I tend to think...

Which of these are beliefs rather than facts?

- **Permanent language** ("I always, never, can't...")
- **Identity statements** ("I'm bad at...")
- **Comparison** ("Everyone else...")
- **Hopelessness** ("It's too late;" "I'll never...")

Limiting Belief #1:

Limiting Belief #2:

Limiting Belief #3:

Part 2: Question Your Beliefs

Work through these questions for each belief.

→ Belief #1:

Is this actually true, or does it simply feel true?

What evidence supports this belief?

What evidence contradicts it, even evidence I usually ignore?

Would I say this to a friend, or only to myself?

What would I believe instead if I didn't believe this?

____

____

→ Belief #2:

Is this actually true, or does it simply feel true?

____

____

What evidence supports this belief?

____

____

What evidence contradicts it, even evidence I usually ignore?

____

____

Would I say this to a friend, or only to myself?

____

____

What would I believe instead if I didn't believe this?

____

____

→ Belief #3:

Is this actually true, or does it simply feel true?

____

____

What evidence supports this belief?

____

____

What evidence contradicts it, even evidence I usually ignore?

____

____

Would I say this to a friend, or only to myself?

____

____

What would I believe instead if I didn't believe this?

____

____

Part 3: Reframe Your Beliefs

Example:

- **Old belief:** "I'm bad with money."
- **Reframe:** "I'm learning about money" or "I haven't been taught this yet" or "I need more practice at handling money.

→ Belief #1 *(my old belief):*

My reframe:

____

____

→ Belief #2 *(my old belief):*

My reframe:

____

____

→ Belief #3 *(my old belief):*

My reframe:

____

____

Part 4: Create New Evidence

The belief I want to change:

____

____

One small action I'll take this week:

____

____

The new evidence this will create:

____

____

When I'll do it:

____

____

Part 5: Track Your Shifts Over the Next Month

Each time you catch yourself thinking an old limiting belief and you then successfully reframe it, mark a checkbox below.

Week 1	[ ]	[ ]	[ ]	[ ]	[ ]
Week 2	[ ]	[ ]	[ ]	[ ]	[ ]
Week 3	[ ]	[ ]	[ ]	[ ]	[ ]
Week 4	[ ]	[ ]	[ ]	[ ]	[ ]

What I notice after one month:

____

____

Lucas says: "Looking honestly at the stories you tell yourself is harder than it sounds. Doing it means you're already thinking differently."

Interlude: You Are Not Broken

A moment before we go further.

You are not broken. Not because your situation is hard, and not because you've done anything wrong. Struggling with money is not evidence of personal failure. It is part of being human in a complicated world.

My husband, Dave, and I came from very different money stories. He had worked multiple jobs, lived at home through college, and built solid savings along the way. I had worked hard, too. I walked into our marriage with student debt and nowhere near the financial foundation he had. Neither story was right or wrong—but they were different.

When those two stories came together, we struggled. We earned good salaries, but by the end of the month, it often felt like the money had disappeared. We told ourselves we understood our finances. In reality, we were guessing, and it wasn't working.

It wasn't because we were irresponsible or didn't care. We hadn't learned yet how to see and relate to money clearly together, and our different starting points made it harder to talk about it.

Sometimes what looks like a personal problem is really a clarity problem.

Most of us were never taught how money works. We were expected to figure it out as we went, often under pressure, often in silence, and usually while comparing ourselves to people we didn't fully understand. So when things feel confusing or tight, it's easy to turn that confusion into a personal conclusion: something must be wrong with me.

Confusion is what happens when learning is missing. It's not a flaw; it's a gap.

Struggling with money does not mean you are irresponsible, and it does not mean you lack discipline or don't care. Many people who are struggling are working hard, making difficult tradeoffs, and managing more than most people can see from the outside. What gets labeled as "making bad decisions" is often someone doing the best they can with limited information, limited margin, and constant pressure. That's not failure. That's effort in a tough situation, and there is a real difference between the two.

Every habit you have about money made sense at the time you learned it. Not looking at your bank account may have reduced anxiety. Focusing only on today may have helped you cope. Putting things off may have felt like the only option. Those weren't mistakes. They were strategies that got you this far. Some of them may not serve you as well going forward, and that's fine. You don't need to judge them. You can simply update them.

Progress doesn't start with shame. It starts with seeing clearly. When you stop asking "What's wrong with me?" and start asking "What's going on here?" something shifts. You begin to notice patterns. You start to see what you haven't been taught yet. You realize there are skills you can learn, and skills can be built with practice and time.

Managing money is a skill, and like anything else, it improves with practice, feedback, and time. There is no final exam. There is only progress, and you are already doing that.

Before we move on, read this sentence slowly.

You are not broken.

You don't have to prove it, you don't have to earn it, you don't have to fix yourself first. If there's a thought you've been carrying, something that sounds more like a conclusion than a fact, you can set it down here. You don't need to carry it with you.

Let that be your starting point. When you're ready, turn the page.

Lucas says: "You don't need to fix yourself before you start. You start, and the fixing happens along the way."

CHAPTER 5

Your CAM Check-In: A Snapshot of Where You Are Right Now

You've taken a close look at how money feels, the stories you tell yourself, and why struggle isn't a character flaw.

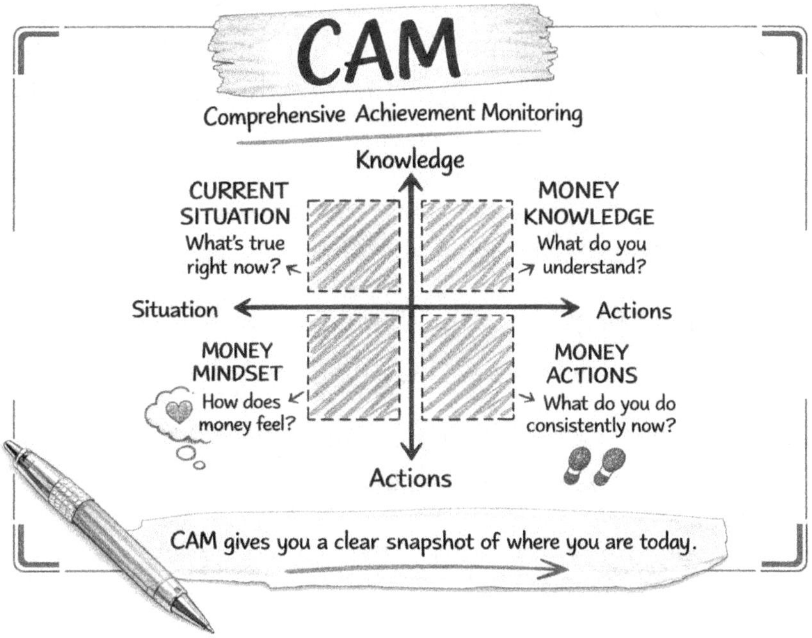

What Is CAM?

CAM stands for **Comprehensive Achievement Monitoring**, and it started in a band room.

Long before I ever taught a financial class, I was taught junior high band. Nearly 80 students were in the room at the same time, with brass warming up, flutes quietly running scales, and percussion trying things out that didn't always match anything else. It was a little chaotic, and I loved it, though loving it didn't make it simple.

With that many students, I couldn't always tell who really understood the music and who was only getting by. Some students looked confident but were guessing. Others were struggling quietly and didn't want to raise their hand and say, "I don't get this."

I created a simple system, not for a grade or to impress anyone. It gave each student a way to check in with themselves, to see clearly what they understood, what they were unsure about, and where they needed a little more attention.

It wasn't about being right or wrong. It was simply a snapshot.

Years later, when I began teaching financial workshops, I saw the same thing. Adults weren't lacking ability; they were lacking clarity.

Everyone had a different story with money, but very few people could answer a simple question: "Where am I right now?"

I brought the same idea into this work.

Why CAM Matters

Managing money can feel overwhelming, not because it's impossible, but because nobody ever really taught you how to look at it. So instead, most people avoid it, guess at it, or react to it.

The CAM Check-In gives you a chance to pause and take an honest look at your financial life. No pressure, no judgment, and no need to have everything figured out first.

Think of it as a snapshot, not a score or a label, but a clear picture of where you are today so you can see where you're headed next.

When you can see your patterns, it becomes much easier to change direction.

The Four Parts of CAM

The CAM Check-In looks at four areas of your financial life.

1. Your Current Situation

This is what's true right now: money coming in, money going out, the accounts you use, and how clear things feel day to day. It doesn't have to be perfect, but you must be real.

2. Your Money Knowledge

This is what you understand about how money works: how accounts work, how interest works, what credit is, and how financial decisions affect you. Gaps here are normal, and everyone has them.

3. Your Money Mindset

This is how you think and feel about money: whether you tend to avoid it or face it, whether you feel stuck or capable, and whether you believe things can get better. This part matters more than most people realize.

4. Your Money Actions

This is what you need to do: save, spend, pay bills, and handle the small daily choices that add up over time. These are the habits that shape everything.

Before You Begin

This is not about getting a high score. It's about being honest.

Some questions may not fully apply to your life yet, and that's okay. Answer based on what's true for you right now.

You are starting from where you are, and that is the right place to begin.

WORKBOOK: CHAPTER 5

YOUR CAM CHECK-IN

This isn't a test. It's a snapshot you'll use to measure your progress over time. Some of these may not fully apply yet. That's okay. Answer based on what's true for you right now.

How to Rate Yourself: *Circle one number for each statement:*

1 = Not true at all **| 2 =** A little true **| 3 =** Sometimes true
4 = Mostly true **| 5 =** Very true

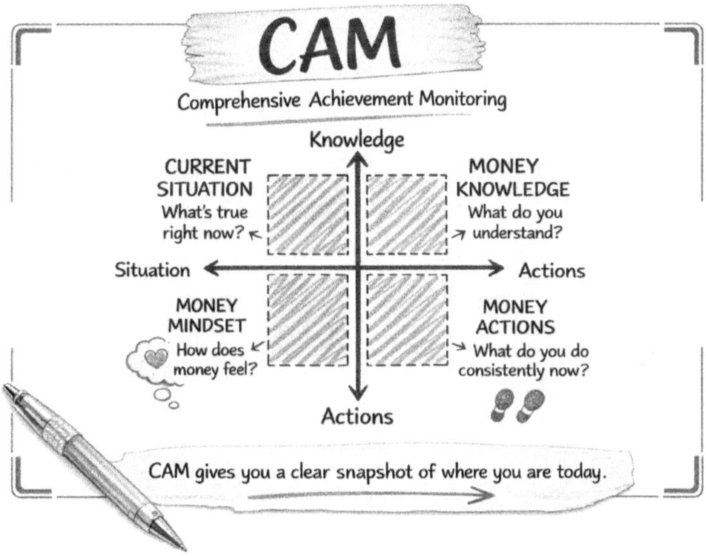

Part 1: Your Current Situation

1. I have a sense of how much money comes in from things like allowance, gifts, or a job.	1 · 2 · 3 · 4 · 5
2. I have a sense of where my money goes, such as food, clothes, subscriptions, or going out.	1 · 2 · 3 · 4 · 5
3. I have a bank account I use, such as a checking or savings account.	1 · 2 · 3 · 4 · 5
4. I check my balance regularly, whether through an app, online, or at the bank.	1 · 2 · 3 · 4 · 5
5. I have a sense of whether I'm spending more or less than I have.	1 · 2 · 3 · 4 · 5
6. I understand what I actually take home from a paycheck after taxes and deductions.	1 · 2 · 3 · 4 · 5
7. I know if I owe money, such as a credit card balance, student loan, or money borrowed.	1 · 2 · 3 · 4 · 5
8. I feel some level of clarity about my money right now, even if it's still developing.	1 · 2 · 3 · 4 · 5
9. I know who I owe and when payments are due, such as credit cards, loans, or other bills.	1 · 2 · 3 · 4 · 5
10. I have a basic understanding of what a credit score is and why it matters.	1 · 2 · 3 · 4 · 5
Section Score (add your numbers 10–50)	**_____ / 50**

Part 2: Your Money Knowledge

1. I understand the difference between a checking account and a savings account.	1 · 2 · 3 · 4 · 5
2. I understand how interest works when saving money or borrowing money.	1 · 2 · 3 · 4 · 5
3. I understand what a credit score is and how it can affect things like loans or renting.	1 · 2 · 3 · 4 · 5
4. I understand how student loans work and what I need to pay attention to.	1 · 2 · 3 · 4 · 5
5. I understand what a simple plan for spending money looks like.	1 · 2 · 3 · 4 · 5
6. I understand how money can grow over time through saving or investing.	1 · 2 · 3 · 4 · 5
7. I understand the difference between using a debit card and a credit card.	1 · 2 · 3 · 4 · 5
8. I know what renters insurance is and what it covers.	1 · 2 · 3 · 4 · 5
9. I understand that there are ways to save and invest for the future, such as a 401(k) or IRA.	1 · 2 · 3 · 4 · 5
10. I understand how to read a basic pay stub and what the different parts mean.	1 · 2 · 3 · 4 · 5

Section Score (add your numbers 10–50) ______ **/ 50**

Part 3: Your Money Mindset

1. I believe I can improve my money situation over time.	1 · 2 · 3 · 4 · 5
2. When I think about money, I feel more curious than stressed.	1 · 2 · 3 · 4 · 5
3. I am willing to look at my account or money situation, even if it feels uncomfortable.	1 · 2 · 3 · 4 · 5
4. I believe past mistakes with money do not define my future.	1 · 2 · 3 · 4 · 5
5. I feel capable of learning what I don't yet know about money.	1 · 2 · 3 · 4 · 5
6. I am aware of how often I compare myself to others when it comes to money.	1 · 2 · 3 · 4 · 5
7. I believe small steps can make a real difference over time.	1 · 2 · 3 · 4 · 5
8. I feel some sense of hope about my financial future.	1 · 2 · 3 · 4 · 5
9. I tend to think things through before spending money.	1 · 2 · 3 · 4 · 5
10. I believe I deserve to feel stable and at peace with my money.	1 · 2 · 3 · 4 · 5

Section Score (add your numbers 10–50) ______ **/ 50**

Part 4: Your Money Actions

1. I have some money set aside for unexpected expenses, like a car repair.	1 · 2 · 3 · 4 · 5
2. I pay bills on time, such as a phone bill, subscription, fees or credit card bills.	1 · 2 · 3 · 4 · 5
3. I keep track of my spending in some way, such as using an app, keeping notes, or checking my account.	1 · 2 · 3 · 4 · 5
4. I have some savings, even if it's a small amount set aside over time.	1 · 2 · 3 · 4 · 5
5. I think carefully before taking on debt for things I don't truly need.	1 · 2 · 3 · 4 · 5
6. I look at my account activity regularly, such as reviewing transactions or balances.	1 · 2 · 3 · 4 · 5
7. I have something I'm saving for, like a car, school expenses, travel, or something important to me.	1 · 2 · 3 · 4 · 5
8. I make intentional choices about what I spend money on, such as needs versus wants.	1 · 2 · 3 · 4 · 5
9. I ask questions or look for reliable information when I'm unsure about money.	1 · 2 · 3 · 4 · 5
10. I am taking steps to improve my money situation right now, even if they are small.	1 · 2 · 3 · 4 · 5

Section Score (add your numbers 10–50) **______ / 50**

Your Total CAM Snapshot
Add your four section scores together (40–200): ________

- **40–80** → Just Starting
- **81–120** → Building Awareness
- **121–160** → Developing Confidence
- **161–200** → Making a strong Foundation

The total matters less than the pattern across the four areas. That pattern shows you where to focus next.

What surprised me:

____

____

One area where I'm stronger than I thought:

____

____

One area where I want to grow:

____

____

One small step I can take this week:

____

____

Keep this CAM Check-In. In six months, take it again. You'll see progress you might not notice day to day. Even small changes count. Progress doesn't have to be loud to be real.

CHAPTER 6

The 10 Money Realities: Read This Before You Try to "Fix" Anything

Honesty without context can quietly turn into self-blame. Before we talk about plans, habits, or strategies, we need to get grounded in what is actually true.

This chapter is not about mindset or motivation. It is about reality, the money truths most people don't learn early enough, the ones that explain why things feel hard even when you are trying your best.

The Money Reality Check

A lot of what people believe about money is not actually true. It is just what looks true from the outside.

The following realities are not excuses you need to overcome. They are truths that deserve to be named out loud.

Here are 10 important Reality points:

Reality #1: You might not have room to save right now. If most of your income goes to rent, food, transportation, and minimum loan payments, advice like "just save more" doesn't help. Sometimes survival is the strategy, and that is enough for right now.

Reality #2: Your "want" spending might be the thing keeping you sane. If eating out once in a while with friends is your only social spending, and everything else goes to needs, that is not frivolous. Mental health matters as much as financial health.

Reality #3: A lot of traditional financial advice assumes privilege you might not have. "Sell something to raise money" assumes you own something worth selling. "Work on campus" assumes those jobs are available to you. "Move somewhere cheaper" assumes you have money to move. When advice doesn't fit your reality, that's a problem with the advice—not with you.

Reality #4: Some people are one emergency away from crisis. Without savings, one flat tire, a medical bill, or an unexpected fee can make you spiral into debt and months of stress. Any book that ignores this is not speaking to real life.

Reality #5: Social media shows lifestyles, not bank balances. What looks like success on a screen often hides debt, stress, or family money behind it. Your path is yours, and it doesn't need to look like anyone else's.

Reality #6: Many people who look "successful" live paycheck to paycheck. Income and financial security are not the same thing. A higher salary with higher spending is just a more expensive version of survival mode.

Reality #7: Student loans can feel suffocating, and that is not being overly dramatic. If much of your paycheck goes to loans, you are being accurate when you say you can't save. That is math, not an excuse.

Reality #8: Financial stress affects your whole life. Money stress affects your sleep, your health, your relationships, your focus, and your ability to make good decisions. It touches almost everything.

Reality #9: Advice that worked in one decade doesn't always work in the next. Affordable college, lower housing costs, and guaranteed pensions were real advantages for earlier generations. Today's conditions are different. The goal is learning to think clearly about money, not following a script written for someone else's life.

Reality #10: Both present-you and future-you matter. Advice that says "sacrifice now, enjoy later" misses something important: you have to get through now to reach later. Balance matters more than extremes.

These realities don't excuse you from making choices. They make sure the choices you make are grounded in what is true.

WORKBOOK: CHAPTER 6

THE MONEY REALITY CHECK

Set a timer for five minutes. Write without stopping, without editing, and without worrying about how it sounds.

Start with: *When I think about my financial reality, not what I wish were true, here's what's real for me...*

When you're done, don't judge what you wrote, but be sure to notice it. Keep this. It is your truth, and it is valid.

END OF PART 1

What Happens Next

You've completed Part 1, both the reading and the reflection. That takes courage.

You now have:

- A clear picture of your whole life.
- An honest awareness of how your money feels right now.
- Insight into the stories you've been telling yourself.
- A complete CAM snapshot of your starting point.
- Context for why money feels overwhelming, and why that is not your fault.

You've built a strong foundation. In Part 2, we shift from understanding your present to shaping your future.

PART 2

Where Are You Going?

Vision and Goals

START SMART
Crew

CHAPTER 7

Meet Your Guides: The Start Smart Crew

Now that you know where you're standing, let me introduce you to some guides who will help you think through where you're going.

Throughout this book, you'll meet a group of young adults who are like you. They have different backgrounds, different personalities, and different paths. They aren't experts or perfect, and they are figuring things out in real time.

Each member of the Start Smart Crew represents a way of thinking about money and with life. You'll see them in stories, in reflection prompts, and in short reminders along the way.

You don't need to identify with all of them, but you'll probably recognize yourself in one or more. Think of them as guides that you learn from, not rules you follow. They're here to strengthen your judgment, not replace it.

How the Crew Shows Up in This Book

The Start Smart Crew will appear throughout the rest of the book. Sometimes you'll see them in stories and examples. Other times you'll find them in margin notes and reflection prompts, offering short reminders of different ways to think through challenges.

The goal isn't to copy what someone else did. It's to learn how to think through your own choices, given the life you're actually living. That's what the Start Smart Crew is here to help you do.

This chapter is about getting to know your guides. There are no exercises here, just introductions. As you read through the rest of the book and the Crew appears in stories and prompts, you'll naturally connect with the ones who feel most like you. Keep them in mind as you move forward.

The Start Smart Crew

Maya (Courage)

The one who starts before she feels ready. Maya reminds you that you're allowed to choose what makes sense for you, even when others are doing something flashier.

Maya says: "Does this actually make sense for me?"

Owen (Clarity)

Thoughtful and calm, cutting through noise. Owen helps you focus on what actually matters before making a decision.

Owen says: "Is this aligned with what I value, or am I trying to impress someone else?"

Aalaya (Goals)

Determined and visionary. Aalaya turns hopes into a direction worth following.

Aalaya says: "What am I aiming for right now?"

Riley (Common Sense)

Curious and practical, asking the simple questions. Riley keeps you grounded when emotions run high.

Riley says: "Does this really make sense? What simple system could make this easier on me?"

Noor (Values)

Grounded and intentional. Noor lets values guide her decisions, even when others don't understand.

Noor says: "Does this reflect who I want to be?"

Jordan (Balance)

Aware of the big picture and how everything connects, Jordan knows that money isn't separate from the rest of your life.

Jordan says: "What's the real cost, not just in dollars?"

Lin (Time Perspective)

Steady and forward-looking, understanding the power of starting early. Lin reminds you that small actions today create big results later.

Lin says: "What will 'future me' thank me for?"

Lucas (Responsibility)

Warm and steady, owning choices without shame. Lucas shows that taking ownership is how growth happens.

Lucas says: "What can I learn from this?"

Sofia (Belief)

Optimistic and encouraging. Sofia is the voice that says keep going. She believes you have more going for you than you think.

Sofia says: “What’s already working that I can build on?”

Diego (Commitment)

Reliable and consistent, focused on showing up even when things feel boring or hard. Diego knows that small, steady steps beat big bursts of effort that fade.

Diego says: “What can I keep doing, even on hard days?”

CHAPTER 8

Clear the Path: Make the Right Choice the Easy Choice

Now that you've met the Crew, let me give you a simple tool they all use when big decisions come up. Whether it's Maya starting something new, Owen cutting through the noise, or Riley checking whether something makes sense, they all follow the same basic process. That process keeps them from reacting under stress or pressure, and helps them make choices that actually fit their lives.

Use a "Study, Think, Decide" Approach

Life is full of big choices: a new job offer, a big purchase, signing a lease for the first time. Before you make any financial decision, use this simple three-step method: Study, Think, Decide.

STUDY

Before you act, learn. Never sign, spend, or commit to something you don't fully understand. That means doing your homework first: look up the facts, ask questions, and gather information about your specific situation.

Researching a used car? Get the numbers. Considering a credit card? Read the terms. Ask yourself: What are the facts? What's the best that could happen? What's the worst? Know what you're dealing with before you make a move.

THINK

This is the step most people skip, and it's the most important. Once you have the facts, sit with them. How do they fit your life and your goals right now?

If you're thinking about a big purchase, ask yourself: What am I giving up to make this happen? If you're considering a new opportunity, ask: Does this actually align with what matters to me, not what sounds really good today? This is where facts turn into a real decision that fits your life. Don't rush it.

DECIDE

You've done the research. You've thought it through. Now it's time to act. Instead of letting the facts float around in your head, make a clear decision, write it down, and take one real action today. Not "someday."

Deciding to open a savings account? Do it now. Deciding to pass on that impulse buy? Write down your reason and stick to it. Once you've walked through Study, Think, Decide, the next step is to make it easier to follow through on your decision.

YOUR TURN: STUDY, THINK, DECIDE

Pick a real money decision you're facing right now or one coming up soon. It could be big (a car, a job offer, moving out) or small (a subscription, a new piece of clothing, or a purchase you keep putting off). Walk through all three steps below.

My decision or situation:

____

____

____

____

STEP 1: *STUDY*

Facts I already have:

____

____

Questions I still need to answer:

____

____

Best-case scenario:

____

____

Worst-case scenario:

____

____

STEP 2: *THINK*

What am I giving up if I do this? (opportunity cost):

____

____

Does this line up with my goals? Yes / No / Not sure — here's why:

____

____

One thing that's making me hesitate or feel pressure:

____

____

STEP 3: *DECIDE*

My decision:

____

____

The one action I will take today:

____

____

Date I'll do it by:

____

____

Remember: the goal isn't a perfect decision. It's a thoughtful one, made by you, for you.

From the Classroom

I had a trumpet player in my third-period class who was genuinely talented but consistently unprepared. Every Tuesday we had the same conversation. I asked, "Did you practice this week?" His answer: "I meant to, but I kept forgetting."

He wasn't lazy. He was a busy eighth grader with sports, homework, and a locker on the other side of the building. His trumpet stayed in its case in the band room because carrying it home felt like one more thing to deal with. By the time he remembered he was supposed to practice, it was already 10 p.m., and the moment had passed.

We didn't have another conversation about trying harder. We built a system. He started taking the trumpet home every Monday, whether he felt like it or not. Every night he put a sticky note on his desk lamp, the one already in his line of sight, that said: practice happens before screens.

Within a month, he was one of the most prepared players in the section. Nothing changed about his intentions. Everything that changed was about his environment.

**You don't need more discipline.
You need a better setup that fits real life.**

Why Willpower Isn't the Answer

That trumpet player didn't need a lecture on trying harder. He needed one small change to his setup. Money works the same way.

A lot of people think money problems come from a lack of willpower. They think if they tried harder, stayed motivated longer, or cared more, things would improve. The truth people do better when the path is clear, when good choices are easier than hard ones, and when simple systems quietly do the work in the background.

Where Friction Hides

Friction is anything that makes the right decision harder than it needs to be. It's not dramatic, and it doesn't announce itself. It shows up as a bill you keep meaning to set to "autopay," an account you avoid opening because you're not sure what you'll find, or a savings transfer you've been meaning to set up since January. Friction is the gap between what you intend to do and what actually happens.

The good news is that friction isn't a character flaw. It's a design problem, and design problems can be fixed.

What "Clearing the Path" Actually Means

Clearing the path means finding where money decisions feel unnecessarily hard and gently making them easier. That might mean fewer decisions, fewer chances to forget, and fewer moments of stress or panic.

- **Owen (Clarity)** helps you see exactly what's blocking you. Not just "handling money feels hard," but the specific thing that keeps not getting done.
- **Riley (Common Sense)** helps you build a system so the easy choice becomes the default.
- **Diego (Commitment)** reminds you that a boring system you

stick with beats a brilliant plan you abandon.

Small Systems Beat Big Intentions

Here's what that looks like in practice:

- Set up automatic transfers so savings happen before you can spend the money.
- Pick one consistent day each week to check in on your money. Ten minutes, same time each week.
- Keep a running list of three financial priorities, nothing more.
- Aim for fewer accounts, not more. Simplicity is easier to maintain.
- Build one default decision so you're not choosing from scratch every time.

The goal isn't to optimize everything.
It's to make follow-through easier than avoidance.

Diego (Commitment) reminds you: "What can I keep doing, even on hard days?" That's really what clearing the path is all about. Fixing it rarely requires a better version of yourself. It only requires a better setup.

WORKBOOK: CHAPTER 8

CLEAR THE PATH

Your Turn: *Clear One Obstacle*

You don't need to clear the whole path today. Just take one step.

Think about your money situation right now. Where does friction show up most often?

One money decision that feels harder than it needs to be is:

____

____

Which guide could help here? Circle the one that fits:

- **Owen (Clarity) —** *Do I need to simplify?*
- **Riley (Common Sense) —** *Do I need a system?*
- **Diego (Commitment) —** *Do I need consistency instead of intensity?*

One small change I could make to clear the path is:

____

____

When I'll do it:

____

____

CHAPTER 9

Define Your Freedom: What Are You Aiming For Right Now?

By now, you've done real work. You've honestly assessed where you are, determined what's true, and recognized the beliefs that might be holding you back. You've taken a clear snapshot of your current situation, met the Start Smart Crew, and begun clearing the path so it's easier to make good choices.

This chapter asks a different question: not "What should I do?" but "What am I aiming for?"

It's about defining freedom, not in a vague "someday" way, but in a way that fits where you are right now.

Freedom Comes Before Goals

Freedom gives goals their meaning. Without it, goals often become pressure.

Most people jump straight to goals: save more, earn more, pay off debt by a certain date. Those instincts aren't wrong, but if freedom isn't part of the picture, goals can quietly become another source of stress. When you start by defining what freedom means to you, the goals that follow actually matter.

What Freedom Is (and Isn't)

Freedom doesn't mean having unlimited money, never worrying again, or having everything figured out. It is usually much simpler: having breathing room and fewer late-night worries, making choices without panic, and being able to say yes or no without that knot of stress in your stomach.

Freedom changes as life changes. What that means at 18 isn't what it means at 28. What it means when you're barely getting by isn't what it means when you're building toward something new.

Freedom Is Seasonal

Right now, your version of freedom might mean (1) paying for your basics without anxiety, (2) not overdrawing your account, 3) keeping your bills in order, and (4) feeling steady instead of reactive.

Later, it might mean saving regularly, paying down debt, taking a well-thought-out risk, or having options you didn't have before.

You don't have to choose the final version, but you do need to define this one.

Lin (Time Perspective) asks a good question: "What will 'future me' thank me for?"

Before you narrow your focus, it helps to check the questions you're asking yourself. When you're stressed about money, it is easy to fall into questions like: *"Why am I so bad with money?"* or *"Why does everyone else seem to be doing better than me?"* Those questions don't lead to clarity. They lead to feeling stuck.

Better Questions Lead You Forward

Try asking these instead:

- What would my life look like if I felt in control of my money?
- What's one thing that would make the biggest difference right now?
- What am I aiming for, not in ten years, but right now?

WORKBOOK: CHAPTER 9

DEFINE YOUR FREEDOM

Your Turn: Define Freedom (The Telescope)

Set a timer for three to five minutes and write nonstop. Don't edit and don't overthink.

Your answer might be simple. It might surprise you. It might change later. All of that is okay.

For me, financial freedom right now looks like . . .

One More Question (Aalaya)

After you write, read it again with fresh eyes. Ask yourself:

- What theme keeps showing up?
- What would make the biggest difference right now?
- What feels like relief instead of pressure?

If one thing improved over the next six months, you'd feel more in control of where you're headed. What is that one thing for you? This isn't a lifetime commitment. It's a directional choice, and direction is powerful.

CHAPTER 10

Goals That Pull You Forward: Turning Vision Into Direction

You've defined what freedom looks like for you right now, and identified what would make the biggest difference in the next six months. Now it's time to turn that clarity into direction with goals that connect to what you genuinely care about.

Aalaya (Goals) reminds you: "What am I aiming for right now? Writing it down turns hopes into direction."

Why Most Goals Don't Work

Most goal-setting fails because the goals aren't really yours. They come from someone else's expectations, they're too vague to act on, or they have nothing to do with what you actually care about.

Sometimes those borrowed goals come from family or cultural expectations that genuinely matter to you, and that's worth paying attention to. The real question is whether this goal fits your life right now, not whether the source of it is valid. If it truly fits, own it. If it's someone else's goal with your name on it, you're allowed to walk away from it.

When goals feel disconnected from your actual life and values, they become another source of pressure. You don't need that.

Three Goal Timeframes

Think of your goals in three timeframes. You're not locking in your whole future; you're giving yourself a flexible map.

1-Year Goals

What needs to happen this year? These goals are specific and achievable, and they directly support your current definition of freedom. For example: "Build a $1,000 emergency fund" or "Pay off my credit card."

3-Year Goals

What becomes possible if you stay consistent? These goals are more aspirational but still grounded. They assume you'll build on your one-year progress. For example: "Have three months of expenses saved" or "Be debt-free except for student loans."

5-Year Goals

What does the bigger picture look like? These goals are broader and more flexible. They help you stay oriented even as the details change. For example: "Feel confident managing money" or "Have enough breathing room to take career risks."

You don't need perfect answers, but you do need a direction.

Later in this chapter, you'll also sketch a 10-year picture. Think of it less as a detailed plan, and more as a sense of the kind of life you want to be able to choose.

What Goals Look Like Across Different Paths

Here are examples of what goals across the three timeframes can look like, depending on where you're headed right now. These are examples, not templates. Use them to spark your thinking, not to copy someone else's direction. Your path might not match any of these exactly, and that's fine. Take what fits and leave the rest.

4-Year College Path

- **1 Year:** Graduate with less than $500 in credit card debt.
- **3 Years:** Finish school with a part-time job that covers your living expenses.
- **5 Years:** Land a job in your field and build a three-month emergency fund.
- **10 Years:** Have the life you want with financial stability.

Trade or Technical Path

- **1 Year:** Complete your program and pass your certification exam.
- **3 Years:** Work full-time in your trade with your startup tools and equipment paid off.
- **5 Years:** Have enough saved to consider starting your own business.
- **10 Years:** Have a job you care about, with a lifestyle you can afford.

Straight to Work

- **1 Year:** Cover your own bills without family help.
- **3 Years: Have** $2,000 saved with no high-interest debt.
- **5 Years:** Feel like you have choices, not just obligations.
- **10 Years:** Have real options, financially stable with room to decide.

A Note on the 10-Year Timeframe

You'll notice the 10-year entries look a little different. That's on purpose. At this point in your life, a 10-year picture isn't really a financial goal. It's more of a life picture: relationships, family, where you want to live, what kind of stability you're building.

Your goals are worth sketching, even loosely, because the financial decisions you make in years one through five determine whether that picture becomes possible. You don't have to know exactly what 10 years looks like. Ask yourself: What kind of life do I want to be able to choose? That's enough to start.

Lin (Time Perspective) reminds you: "The decisions you make in years one through five are already building the life you'll have at in ten years. You don't need a perfect plan, but have a direction worth moving toward."

CHAPTER 10 WORKBOOK

Goals That Pull You Forward

Based on what you wrote about freedom, answer these questions.

1-Year Goals

What are 1-3 specific financial goals I want to achieve in the next 12 months that will move me toward financial freedom?

Goal 1: ____

Goal 2: ____

Goal 3: ____

3-Year Goals

If you stay consistent, what 1-3 things will become possible in 3 years?

Goal 1: ____

Goal 2: ____

Goal 3: ____

5-Year Goals

What will the bigger picture look like 5 years from now?

Goal 1: ____

Goal 2: ____

Goal 3: ____

10-Year Picture (Optional)

You don't need to have this figured out. But if you're ready to sketch it, what kind of life do you want to be able to choose in ten years? Think beyond finances: relationships, family, where you want to live, and what stability means to you. Your picture might include your own stability, your family's, or both. Write what's actually true for you.

In 10 years, I want to be able to:

____

____

Questions to Test Your Goals

Look at what you wrote and ask yourself:

- Does this goal support my current definition of freedom?
- Is this goal mine, or am I trying to meet someone else's expectations?
- Can I break this goal into smaller steps?
- Can I describe what "done" looks like for this goal?
- Is there one action I can take this week toward this goal?

If you can't answer yest to these questions, it's okay to revise your goal. Fewer goals that matter are better than many goals that create pressure.

One action I'll take this week:

____

____

You're not trying to control the entire future. You're giving yourself a clear direction and one next step that keeps the wheel moving.

PART 3

How Will You Get There?

The 10 Principles for Building a Strong Financial Life

Seeing What Others Can't

You have taken an honest look at where you are: your Ferris wheel, your money stories, and the patterns you have been following. You have defined what freedom means to you right now, and you have begun to clear a path so that making good choices feels a little easier.

Now it is time to move forward. The 10 Start Smart Money Principles are not complicated formulas or tricks to get rich quickly. They are basic truths about money that, when practiced consistently, build a solid financial life over time. You do not need to master all 10 at once. Start where you are and build from there.

Each principle features a real story, a KEY INSIGHT, and a Small Step you can take this week. You will also find a "Your Turn" reflection to help you connect each idea to your life.

You do not need to read all 10 in one sitting. Choose the one that feels most relevant right now. Principles 1, 2, and 4 are good places to start. Try the Small Step, see what happens, and come back for the next one when you are ready.

Maya (Courage) reminds you: "I do not need this to be complicated. I just need to start."

Turn the page to see the **10 Smart Money Principles**

Principle 1: Start Now, Even If It's Small

The best time to start was yesterday. The second-best is today.

Principle 2: Pay Yourself First

'Future You' gets paid before anyone else, automatically and without negotiation.

Principle 3: Let Time and Consistency Do the Heavy Lifting

Small habits repeated over time beat big, dramatic gestures every time.

Principle 4: Build Your Safety Cushion

Life will break something. The only question is when, not if.

Principle 5: Protect What Matters Most

One unexpected event shouldn't undo years of good choices.

Principle 6: Keep More of What You Earn

Most people don't have an income problem. They have a leak problem: small, unnoticed spending that drains their budget.

Principle 7: Keep It Simple and Know Who Gets Paid

The simpler your money systems, the easier they are to manage, and the clearer it is who benefits from each product you use.

Principle 8: Invest Intelligently with Help You Trust

You don't need to be a genius. You need a simple plan and people who are genuinely on your side.

Principle 9: Teach It Forward

The best way to truly understand something is to teach it to someone else.

Principle 10: Keep a Winning Attitude

Progress beats perfection. Staying curious matters more than feeling ashamed, and showing up consistently will always outrun short bursts of intensity.

PRINCIPLE 1

Start Now, Even If It's Small

Waiting for the perfect time costs more than starting small. The best time to begin was yesterday. The second-best is today.

The most powerful financial move you can make isn't about how much money you have. It's about when you start. A investment of $100 at age 22 will work harder for you than $1,000 invested at age 32. Time is the secret ingredient that turns small actions into big outcomes.

I learned this lesson long before I taught it in a financial workshop. One of the best "teachers" I ever had was a seventh-grade percussionist who could barely keep a steady beat. By ninth grade, he was one of the best young drummers I'd ever seen. His mother told me he'd made a deal with himself in sixth grade: ten minutes of practice every day. Not an hour on Saturdays when he felt motivated. Ten minutes every day. Two years of ten-minute practice sessions.

What he built in those two years, the feel, the timing, the confidence, couldn't have been built any other way. You can't cram it. You can't skip to it. You do have to show up until one day you look up and realize you're already there.

KEY INSIGHT: *That's compound interest in a person. Ten minutes a day, five dollars a paycheck, the amount is almost beside the point.* ***The habit is everything.***

Think of it like planting a tree. On day one, it's only a small sapling, nothing impressive. But give it time, and that sapling becomes shade, shelter, and a legacy.

However small or messy it feels, the answer is to start anyway.

Lin (Time Perspective) asks the question worth sitting with: "What will 'Future me' think of today's choices?"

Why Starting Now Beats Starting Big

Here's what the numbers actually show. Assume a 7% average annual return over 40 years: Maya invested $12,000 and ended up with about $550,000. Jordan invested $39,600—more than three times as much—and ended up with about $309,000.

Starting early beats working harder every time.

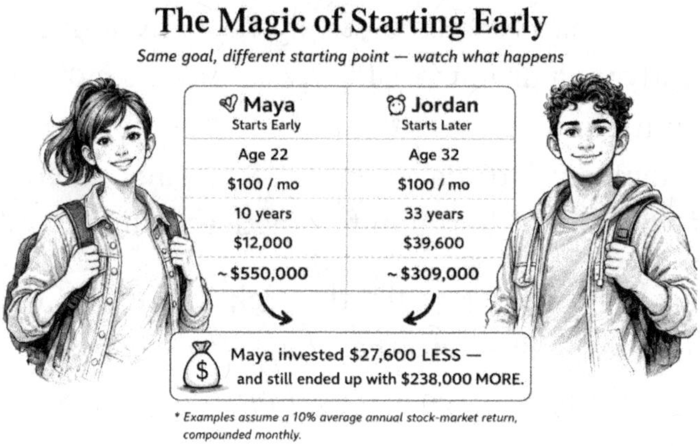

IT WORKS. HERE'S PROOF:

"Kay Hawley inspired me to start planning for my future at age 23. Thirty-two years later, I retired at 55, completely debt-free, and now spend my time doing work I truly enjoy. Her guidance helped shape the course of my life." —Terri Osland, Teacher

How to Actually Start (Right Now)

Step 1: Pick Your Starting Amount

- $5 per week = $260 per year
- $10 per week = $520 per year
- $25 per paycheck (bi-weekly) = $650 per year
- $50 per month = $600 per year

Step 2: Make It Automatic

Open a separate savings account. Set up an automatic transfer for the day after payday. The amount matters less than the habit.

Step 3: Don't Touch It

This money isn't for concerts, coffee, or "emergencies" like a good sale. This is 'Future You' money. Let it sit. Let it grow.

SMALL STEP #1 - START NOW

Do This This Week:

- Open a savings account (if you don't have one).
- Set up a $5, $10, or $25 automatic transfer for the next payday.
- Write down today's date and your starting balance.

Today's date: _____

My starting amount: $_____

My automatic transfer: $_____ every

Your Turn: Reflection Questions

1. What's one reason I've been waiting to start saving?
2. What's the smallest amount I can commit to saving right now?
3. What would it feel like to have $500 saved six months from now?

PRINCIPLE 2

Pay Yourself First

Every paycheck comes with a long list of people waiting to be paid: your landlord, your credit card company, your phone provider, and your student loans. If you let everyone else go first, there is almost never anything left for you at the end.

Paying yourself first means treating your future self like a bill that cannot be skipped—even if it is only $25 per paycheck. It comes before rent, groceries, and the fun stuff. That transfer to savings happens first, automatically, without negotiation, and without guilt.

The "Pay Yourself First" System

Old approach (doesn't work): Get paid → Pay bills → Buy groceries → Go out with friends → Handle unexpected expenses → Save whatever's left (usually nothing)

New approach: Get paid → Automatically transfer savings (before you see it, before you spend it) → Pay bills with what remains → Live on the rest

How Much Should You Pay Yourself?

Start with a percentage, not a dollar amount. As your income grows, your savings grows with it. If 10% isn't possible, start with 5%. If 5% isn't possible, start with 1%. Something always beats nothing.

A Story of Paying Yourself First: *Lucas Makes It Work*

Lucas earns $1,800 a month. After he pays rent, bills, and groceries, money feels tight. Saving feels impossible. He starts small—only 5% of his paycheck, $90 a month, is transferred automatically the day after payday. He never sees it. He never has to decide.

- **Month 1:** It feels strange not having that $90 in checking, but he adjusts.
- **Month 6:** He has $540 saved and feels calmer than he has in years.
- **Year 1:** He increases it to 10%. His savings grow past $1,000.
- **Year 2:** When his roommate moves out without warning, Lucas covers the rent gap without panic, without debt, and without calling his parents.

Lucas didn't wait to make more money. He paid himself first from what he had, and that changed everything.

Lucas (Responsibility) reminds you: "Own it and move forward. You can't change what you haven't saved yet, but you can absolutely change what happens next."

SMALL STEP #2 - PAY YOURSELF FIRST

Do This This Week:

- Calculate 10% of your monthly income,
- Set up an automatic transfer to savings (even if it's less than 10%).
- Schedule the transfer for the day after payday.

I will automatically save $_____ every

Your Turn: Reflection Questions

1. What percentage of my income can I realistically save right now?
2. What's one bill I currently pay that's less important than paying 'Future me'?
3. If I saved $100 a month for a year, what would that $1,200 mean for my life?

PRINCIPLE 3

Let Time and Consistency Do the Heavy Lifting

Small habits repeated over time beat big dramatic gestures every single time. Steady and consistent wins.

Financial success isn't built in a single dramatic moment. It's built on a thousand small, unglamorous, consistent decisions that no one sees or applauds.

You don't need to be brilliant. You simply need to show up, make the steady choice, and let time do the rest.

Diego (Commitment) reminds you: "What can I keep doing, even on hard days? Small, consistent actions add up."

In 30 years of teaching music, and as many years running financial awareness workshops, I have found that the people who succeeded weren't always the most talented or naturally gifted. They were the ones who refused to give up. My best music students showed up to every rehearsal, worked through the hard passages without complaint, and came back the next day after a poor performance without missing a beat. My most successful workshop participants maintained their automatic savings, even when money was tight, and they quietly returned the following year, further ahead than when they left.

What they all had in common was simple: they never gave up. That quality—that quiet determination to keep going when progress is invisible, and nobody is watching—is worth more than talent, more than timing, and more than any single financial decision you will ever make.

Why Consistency Beats Big Dramatic Gestures

The Intense Approach: Save $300 in one month, burn out, give up, and save nothing for the next 11 months. Year total: $300.

The Consistent Approach: Automate saving $150 per month and keep going even when life gets messy. Year total: $1,800.

In one year, the result is six times greater. Consistency is the reason.

Three Ways to Build Consistency (Without Willpower)

Strategy 1: Automate Everything Possible. Automate savings transfers, bill payments, retirement contributions, and extra debt payments. A one-time setup means ongoing consistency.

Strategy 2: Use Habit Stacking. Attach a new habit to something you already do. Every time you get paid, check your savings balance. Every Sunday, review last week's spending for five minutes.

Strategy 3: Track Streaks, Not Perfection. Don't just track how much you saved. Track how many months in a row you saved something. Celebrate your streaks.

SMALL STEP #3 — CONSISTENCY

Do This This Week:

- Check that your automated savings transfer is still running,
- Pick one small money habit to repeat every week for the next month.
- Write down how many months in a row you have saved something, and start your streak count.

My consistency habit:

My streak so far: _____ months

Your Turn: Reflection Questions

1. What's one small money action I could do every week for the next 90 days?
2. What gets in the way of my consistency most often, and what's one way to work around it?
3. What would my savings look like two years from now if I simply kept going?

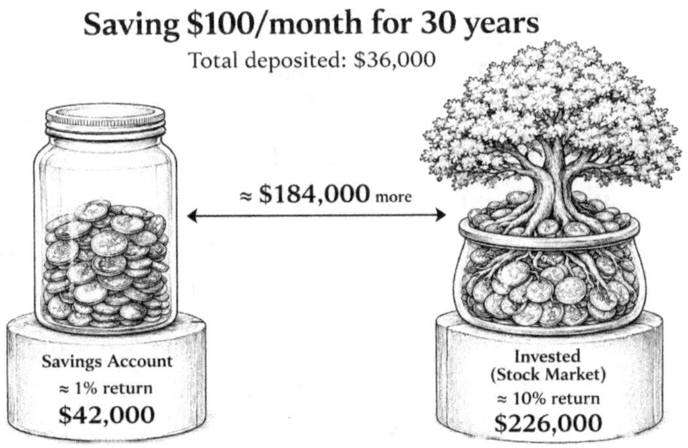

Same saving habit. Different growth engine.
Over time, the engine matters.

PRINCIPLE 4

Build Your Safety Cushion

Life breaks things; that part isn't really optional. What you can influence is how hard a problem hits when it does.

A tire blows, your phone dies, or a tooth suddenly needs attention, and the bill shows up whether you're ready or not. An emergency fund isn't about expecting disaster; it's about accepting that real life has surprises, and you choose to meet them with a little padding. When you have even $500 set aside in a separate savings account, what used to feel like a disaster feels like a manageable problem you can handle.

Jordan (Balance) puts it this way: "Not having this fund costs more than money—it costs peace of mind."

The 3 Layers of Your Safety Net

Layer 1: Breathing Room Fund ($500). This first layer is your small but mighty shield. It covers most everyday emergencies: a surprise bill, a minor car repair, a medical copay, or the cost of replacing something essential that suddenly stops working. The key is that this goal feels reachable in months, not years, so it becomes an early win rather than a lifelong project. Once you're here, you move from "I'm one bad day away from panic" to "I have at least a little space to breathe."

Layer 2: Job Loss Buffer (about $1,500–$2,000). Layer 2 is roughly one month of your basic expenses: housing, food, transportation, and a few essentials. It won't make losing a job easy, but it does give you some time to think, look around, and make clearer choices instead of grabbing the first option out of fear. At this point, you're no longer completely stuck; you can say, "I have a bit of time and a few options," and that changes how every decision feels.

Layer 3: Full Safety Net (3–6 months of expenses). This layer is your longer-term safety net and it usually takes years to build, especially in your 20s when your income and expenses are still shifting. That's perfectly normal. Layers 1 and 2 are designed to handle most of what you're likely to face right now, while you gradually grow this bigger cushion in the background. With a full safety net in place, the feeling shifts from just getting by to "I'm genuinely secure, even when life throws curveballs."

SMALL STEP #4 - BUILD YOUR SAFETY CUSHION

Do This This Week:

- Open a separate savings account to use for emergencies, if you don't already have one.
- Set up your first automatic transfer into that account, choosing an amount that feels realistic for you right now.
- Pause or cancel one thing you pay for automatically, a streaming service, a gaming or music subscription, or an app you barely use, and send that amount to your emergency fund instead.

My Layer 1 goal: $500 by ____________

My automatic savings: $_____ per month

Your Turn: Reflection Questions

1. What's the last "emergency" that caught me off guard? Or, if I haven't had one yet, what's a realistic situation I could imagine showing up?
2. How would my life feel different if I already had $500 set aside right now?
3. What is one expense or subscription I can cut, reduce, or pause to help this fund grow faster?

A Layered Emergency Fund

PRINCIPLE 5

Protect What Matters Most

Guard your credit, your identity, and your insurance. One event shouldn't undo years of good choices.

You can do everything right. Save diligently, invest wisely, budget carefully, and still lose it all if you don't protect your foundation. This principle has two layers: (1) protecting your credit and identity, and (2) safeguarding your life and property with the right insurance.

Noor (Values) reminds you: "Does this reflect who I want to be? Everything I'm working to build deserves to be protected."

Layer 1: Your Credit and Identity

Your credit score follows you everywhere, when renting an apartment, getting a car loan, and sometimes even applying for a job. It's a three-digit number between 300 and 850, and where you fall in that range can save you thousands of dollars over your lifetime, or cost you just as much.

Typical score ranges: 300–579 *Poor* | 580–669 *Fair*
670–739 *Good* | 740–799 *Very Good* | 800–850 *Exceptional*

A good score of 700 or higher opens doors. A lower one closes doors at the worst potential moments, and often for reasons you never see coming.

I think about a young man who came to one of my workshops a few years after landing his first real job. In addition to being sharp and hardworking, he did everything else right. He had tried to rent an apartment near his job, but he was turned down, not because he couldn't afford it, but because his credit score was 520. It was lower than he realized. A couple of missed college payments and a medical bill he'd ignored had followed him in ways he never expected. He lived 40 minutes from his job for another year, spending more on gas than he would have saved on rent, while improving his credit score. "Nobody ever told me that stuff was being tracked," he said. True, nobody had.

Now you know.

Here's what actually moves your score in the right direction. Payment history carries the most weight, paying on time, every time, is the single most important thing you can do. Keeping your credit card balances well below your limit matters too. So does leaving older accounts open, even if you don't use them much, because the length of your credit history counts. Applying for new credit creates a small temporary dip, so resist the urge to open accounts you don't need.

Protecting your identity is as important as building your score. Check your credit report at least once a year at AnnualCreditReport.com. It's free, and it's the only site authorized by federal law. You're entitled to a free report from each of the three major credit bureaus: Equifax, Experian, and TransUnion. Look for accounts you don't recognize. If your information has ever been part of a data breach, consider freezing your credit with all three bureaus. A credit freeze is free; it doesn't affect your score, and it prevents anyone from opening new accounts in your name without your permission.

Layer 2: Insurance

Insurance isn't exciting, but it matters. You're not buying it because you're pessimistic. You're buying it because you're realistic, and because one unexpected event shouldn't be able to undo years of good choices.

I think about a young woman who moved into her first apartment. She was doing everything right, working, saving, and building her independence. One night, a pipe burst in the unit above hers. She woke to water pouring through her ceiling. Her laptop, furniture, and clothes were soaked and ruined, through no fault of her own. She didn't have renters insurance.

It's one of those things that adults assume someone else already told you, but often nobody has. Replacing everything set her back financially for months. Renters insurance typically costs less than a cup of coffee a week, yet most young people skip it simply because nobody ever put it in front of them. Now it's in front of you. Know what's out there, and get it when the timing is right.

Health Insurance: Medical bills without coverage can be enormous. If your employer offers it, enroll. If you're under 26, you may be able to stay on a parent's plan. If not, explore your state's Health Insurance Marketplace for options available.

Auto Insurance: If you drive, this insurance is usually legally required. It protects you if you cause an accident or your car is damaged. Don't skip buying it.

Renters Insurance: This insurance covers your belongings if they're stolen, damaged, or destroyed, even when it's not your fault. It is often surprisingly affordable. Get it as soon as you have your own place.

Life Insurance: If someone depends on your income, term life insurance protects them if something happens to you. It's more affordable when you're young and healthy.

Disability Insurance: If you can't work due to illness or injury, this helps you pay your bills. Many employers offer it, and it's worth asking about when you start a job.

SMALL STEP #5 - PROTECT WHAT MATTERS MOST

Do This This Week:

- Check your credit score through your bank app or a free trusted site like Credit Karma.
- Set up autopay for at least the minimum payment on all your bills and on-time payment history is the fastest way to build and protect your score.
- Visit AnnualCreditReport.com and pull your free report; then look for anything that doesn't belong.
- Make a quick insurance checklist: what do you have, and what's still missing?

My current credit score: ____________

My credit goal: ____________

Your Turn: Reflection Questions

1. When did I last check my credit score, and what do I think it actually is right now?
2. Which insurance types do I currently have, and which do I still need?
3. If a pipe bursta above my apartment tonight, how protected will I be?

PRINCIPLE 6

Keep More of What You Earn

Most people do not simply have an income problem. They have a leak problem.

Small, often invisible, recurring expenses drain $5 here, $10 there, $15 over there until hundreds, sometimes thousands, of dollars disappear each month. Keeping more of what you earn is not about deprivation. It is about noticing where your money quietly slips away, and deciding what you want it to do instead.

Riley (Common Sense) reminds you: "Does this really make sense? Or am I just bleeding money on things that do not matter?"

The Four Money Leaks Draining Your Paycheck

Leak 1: The Subscription Leak. Streaming services, music and game subscriptions, apps, and memberships feel small on their own. The average person has more active subscriptions than they realize. The fix: pull up your bank or card app, look for monthly charges, and cancel anything you have not used in the last 30 days. One careful audit can save you hundreds of dollars a year.

Leak 2: The Convenience Leak. Food delivery, drive-thrus, and "I am too tired to cook" decisions add up fast. The fix: reduce friction with simple backup meals and snacks at home. Give yourself a small, planned amount each month for convenience, so it becomes a choice, not your default.

Leak 3: The Invisible Spending Leak. "It is only..." thinking, buying because something is on sale, and paying extra for brand names when you do not really care, all quietly drain your account. The fix: for one week, track every purchase under $20. You cannot change what you never see.

Leak 4: The Lifestyle Inflation Leak. You get a raise or a refund, and your spending rises to match it. Your savings stays the same. The fix: use a simple "raise rule." When extra money comes in, send part of it straight to savings or debt payoff before you see it in checking.

A Starting Point for Where Your Money Goes: The 50/30/20 Framework

Once you start plugging the leaks, a natural question comes up: "If I am not wasting as much, where should my money go?" One simple answer is the 50/30/20 framework. It is not a rulebook, but it is a helpful starting point. It divides your take-home pay into three broad categories.

Needs (about 50%): Things you genuinely cannot skip: housing, utilities, groceries, transportation, minimum loan payments, and health insurance. If your needs regularly take more than 50%, which is common, especially in high-cost-of-living areas or when you are helping family, that is not failure. That is your current reality. Work with the numbers you actually have.

Wants (about 30%): Things that make life enjoyable but could be adjusted if needed: dining out, streaming services, entertainment, hobbies, clothing beyond basics. Wants are not bad, but they are often where leaks like unused subscriptions and convenience spending hide.

Savings and Debt Payoff (about 20%): Your Pay Yourself First transfer, emergency fund contributions, and extra payments beyond the minimums on debt. This category is what builds your future.

Example: If you bring home $2,000 a month:

1. Needs (50%) = $1,000 – housing, groceries, utilities, transportation, loan minimums
2. Wants (30%) = $600 – dining out, subscriptions, entertainment, clothing
3. Savings and Debt Payoff (20%) = $400 – savings transfer, extra debt payments, emergency fund

That is a clean picture on paper. Real life is messier. The framework should adjust to your reality, not the other way around.

Start by looking at what your percentages actually are right now. Most people have never done this calculation. Seeing the numbers clearly, without judgment, is the first step.

Lin (Time Perspective) reminds you: "What will 'Future me' think of today's choices? I want to look back and know I paid attention."

SMALL STEP #6 – KEEP MORE OF WHAT YOU EARN

Do This This Week:

- List every subscription you have (streaming, music, games, apps, memberships).
- Cancel at least one you do not actively use.
- Track your "it is only..." spending for seven days.

Subscription canceled: $_____

Monthly savings: $_____

Annual savings: $_____

Your Turn: Reflection Questions

1. Where is my money leaking right now: subscriptions, convenience, invisible spending, or lifestyle inflation?
2. What is one expense for something I would not even miss if I cut or reduced it?
3. Looking at the 50/30/20 framework, which category feels most out of proportion in my life right now: needs, wants, or savings?

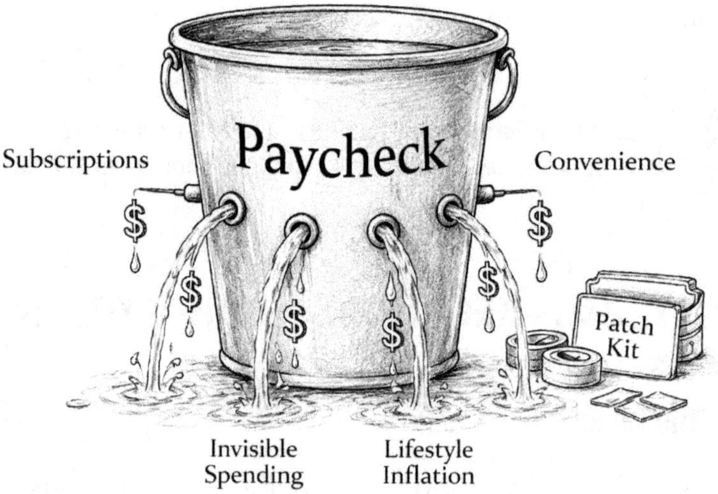

PRINCIPLE 7

Keep It Simple, and Know Who Gets Paid

Complexity costs money, time, and clarity. Simplicity is a strategy.

When your financial life gets complicated, it gets harder to keep up. Keep it simple, and it is easier to manage.

I learned this firsthand when I helped teachers in my school district choose their retirement plan provider. We had options from several investment companies, and they all charged an annual fee based on a percentage of a person's account balance. That sounds reasonable at first, but think it through. The more you save, the more you pay. By the time teachers were close to retirement and finally had real money set aside, they were paying the highest fees of their careers. The people who had done everything right for 30 years were getting charged the most for it. Once you see that, common sense takes over.

We chose the flat-fee option instead. A teacher with $40,000 saved paid the same annual fee as a teacher with $400,000 saved. Simple, fair, and easy to understand. That is the whole point.

That is what "know who gets paid" really means, not in a suspicious way, but in a clear-eyed way. Every time you set up a financial product, a bank account, a credit card, a retirement plan, an investment app, someone is getting paid. Sometimes it is you, sometimes it is them, and sometimes it is both. The question is whether you understand the deal before you say yes. You need to know who gets paid, how much, and how often.

Aalaya (Goals) reminds you: "What am I aiming for right now? A financial life I can actually see and understand. That is a goal worth having."

Owen (Clarity) reminds you: "Is this aligned with what I value? I want to actually understand what I am paying, and I want advice from someone who is genuinely on my side."

What Simple Looks Like

A simple, effective financial setup for many people might look like this:

- One checking account for daily expenses
- One savings account for emergencies
- One retirement account when your job offers it
- Low-cost investments when you are ready
- Only the insurance you actually need

That's really all there is to it. You can see your entire financial picture in under 10 minutes.

As your life gets more complex, you might add a second savings account for a specific goal or an investing app to buy index funds (check out index funds in the tool kit). The goal is still the same: a setup you can explain to a friend in a few sentences without needing a flowchart.

Where to Watch Out

Even with a simple setup, money can quietly leak out in places nobody warned you about. Here are two worth knowing:

Too Many Accounts. Multiple checking accounts and old retirement accounts scattered everywhere create clutter, not organization. Clutter makes it easier to lose track of fees, due dates, and unused services. Consolidate where it makes sense so you are not logging into 12 different places just to see your own money.

High-Fee Investment Products. Ask about fees before you invest. Look for low-cost index funds, and be cautious about anything that has a complicated fee structure you cannot easily explain. If someone is pitching it as "exclusive" or "too good to pass up," that is worth a second look. If in under two minutes you cannot figure out what you are paying, that is a red flag.

Commissioned Salespeople Disguised as Advisors

When pay depends on sales, salespeople sometimes prioritize selling you products over advising you. They may call themselves advisors, but if they earn a commission, their interests and yours may not align. That does not make them bad people. It just means you should ask: "How do you get paid?" If the answer isn't straightforward about money, your intuition should guide you.

When you can, look for fee-only financial advisors or use low-cost platforms from well-known, trusted firms. And when you are just starting out, you usually do not need an advisor at all. A simple index fund and an automatic transfer will get you most of the way.

SMALL STEP #7 – KEEP IT SIMPLE AND KNOW WHO GETS PAID

Your Assignment This Week:

- Look at one financial product you already use, a credit card, a bank account, a retirement account, or an investing app. Find out what fee you pay. Is it a flat fee or a percentage? Do you pay it monthly or annually? If you cannot find the answer in under two minutes, make a note of that. It tells you something.

- Write down every financial account you have: checking, savings, credit cards, apps like Venmo or Cash App, and any old retirement accounts from previous jobs. Can you see all of your money in under five minutes, or does it feel scattered?
- As your financial life grows, keep it simple on purpose. Have one checking account, one savings account, one retirement account when your job offers it, low-cost investments when you are ready, and only the insurance you actually need.

The goal is a financial life simple enough that you can see all of it clearly, anytime you want, and clear enough that you always know who is getting paid.

Your Turn: Reflection Questions

1. How many financial accounts do I have right now? Which ones do I actually use and need?
2. For one product that I already use. Do I know how the person or company offering it gets paid? If not, where can I find out?
3. What is one thing I can simplify this week: close an old account, cancel a product I do not use, or start writing down everything in one place?

PRINCIPLE 8

Invest Intelligently with Help You Trust

You do not need to be a stock market genius. You need a simple plan, steady habits, and guidance from people you can truly trust.

Intelligent investing is not about hot tips or day trading. It is about choosing low-cost index funds, contributing regularly, and letting your money grow over time. Compound interest does the quiet work in the background while you live your life.

Why Investing Matters

The earlier you start, the harder your money works. An investor who begins at age 25 and stops at 35 can sometimes end up with more than someone who waits until age 35 and contributes for the next 30 years. That is the power of compound interest: your money earns returns, and those returns earn returns.

Lin (Time Perspective) reminds you: "What will 'Future me' thank me for? Starting early, even if it is small."

A young woman named Katie came to one of my workshops about 15 years ago. She was in her mid-thirties, had a steady job, and was doing reasonably well, but she had never invested a single dollar. Every time the subject came up, she changed the topic. "That's not for people like me," she told me after the session. "I don't understand any of it, and I don't trust any of it."

We talked for a while after everyone else had left. I didn't explain the market or impress her with the numbers. I asked her one question: "Do you trust your credit union?" She did, so I told her to go in that week, tell them she wanted to open a Roth IRA, put in $25 a month, and choose the simplest broad index fund they offered. Nothing more complicated than that.

She came back to my workshop three years later and pulled me aside. She had never missed a monthly contribution and had increased it twice. Her balance wasn't life-changing yet, but it was real, and more important, the fear was gone. "I don't know why I waited so long," she said. That question stays with me.

Real Investing vs. Hype and Gambling

Right now, young adults see a lot of messages about crypto, meme stocks, and trading apps that promise quick profits. It can feel like everyone else is out there making bold moves on their phone and getting rich doing it.

Real investing usually looks quiet and steady. You choose broad index funds, set up automatic contributions, and let time do most of the work. Gambling dressed up as investing looks like chasing the next big thing, trading constantly, or putting money into something you do not really understand because someone online promised huge returns with almost no risk.

If something feels like gambling dressed up as investing, be skeptical. If someone promises guaranteed high returns, pressures you to act fast, or asks you to send money or crypto to a stranger who will "teach you how to invest," that is a red flag. Legitimate teachers and legitimate companies give you time to think, explain the risks clearly, and never need you to hurry.

The Simple 3-Step Investing Plan

Step 1: Start with Employer Match (If Available). If your job offers a retirement plan with an employer match, contribute at least enough to get the full match. That is money you would not receive any other way, and it is one of the easiest places to start.

Step 2: Open a Roth IRA. Open a Roth IRA at a well-known firm such as Vanguard, Fidelity, or Schwab. Choose one simple, broad stock market index fund, and set up automatic monthly contributions. If you are not sure where to start, a trusted adult, a credit union, or a nonprofit financial counselor can help you get set up. You do not have to figure it out alone.

Step 3: Increase Contributions Over Time. Every time you get a raise, increase your contributions. Each year, try to raise them by a small amount you can stick with.

Diego (Commitment) reminds you: "What can I keep doing, even on hard days? Steady and consistent is how I win."

SMALL STEP #8 - INVEST INTELLIGENTLY

Do This This Week:

- If you have a workplace plan, increase your contribution by 1%.
- If you don't have a retirement account, open a Roth IRA.
- Choose one simple index fund and set up an automatic monthly contribution.

My investment account: ______________

My monthly contribution: ______________

Your Turn: Reflection Questions

1. What is one thing that has been stopping me from investing, and is it still a good enough reason to wait?
2. Who is one person in my life I trust enough to talk to about getting started?
3. If I put just $25 a month into an index fund starting today, where might I be in 10 years? (Hint: more than $5,000, and that is the conservative estimate.)

PRINCIPLE 9

Teach It Forward

The best way to truly understand something is to teach it to someone else.

One of the best ways to change your financial future is to help someone else change theirs. Teaching doesn't have to happen in a classroom; it happens when you explain to a younger sibling why saving matters, when you show a friend how you set up automatic savings, or when you walk someone through why you split rent the way you do.

When you teach financial principles forward, two things happen. (1) you cement your own understanding, and (2) you create a ripple effect that helps someone else avoid mistakes you have already made.

In my thirty years of teaching music, the students who grew the fastest were never the most naturally talented ones; they were the ones I put in charge of helping someone else. I used to pair my strongest players with students who were struggling. Not as tutors exactly, but as section leaders. Their job wasn't to fix anyone; it was simply to sit beside them and play through the music together.

What happened consistently surprised me; the struggling student improved, but the section leader improved more. Explaining a rhythm forces you to feel it differently, and demonstrating a breath technique makes you conscious of something you had been doing on autopilot for years. Teaching it makes you own it in a way that practice alone never has.

I have watched this same pattern play out in every financial awareness workshop I have run. The person who goes home and tells someone else what they learned, even imperfectly, even just one thing, retains it, builds on it, and lives it differently.

You don't have to know everything to start teaching; you just have to know one thing more than the person you're talking to.

Aalaya (Goals) reminds you: "What am I aiming for right now? To understand this well enough to pass it on."

Six Ways to Teach About Money

1. Normalize Money Conversations: Start small by bringing money into everyday conversation. Something as simple as "I recently set up automatic savings. Are you doing anything like that?" goes a long way. When you make money talk normal, others feel safe enough to start learning.
2. Share Your Mistakes: Don't share only your wins; share your losses too, because your mistakes are often someone else's most valuable lessons.
3. Teach Younger Siblings or Relatives: You don't need to sit anyone down for a formal lesson; just share what you are learning as you go, in the same natural way you would tell someone about a good movie or a useful app.
4. Help Friends Make Better Decisions: When a friend is considering a big financial decision, share what you have learned, not as a lecture, but as someone who genuinely cares about how things turn out for them.
5. Model Good Behavior: Silent modeling is still teaching. When you turn down an expensive night out because it is not in your budget, you give others quiet permission to do the same, and that matters more than you might think.

6. Advocate for Financial Literacy: If you see a financial education gap in your school, workplace, or community, say something. Encouraging others to bring personal finance into the conversation, and sharing helpful resources when you find them, are two of the simplest ways to create change.

SMALL STEP #9 – TEACH IT FORWARD

Do This This Week:

- Choose one person who can really use something you have learned.
- Pick one money idea or habit you feel comfortable sharing.
- Share it in a simple way, a quick conversation, a text, or a message.

Person I will teach: ______________________________

Topic I will share: ______________________________

When I will do it: ______________________________

Your Turn: Reflection Questions

1. Who is one person in my life who could benefit from something I have learned?
2. What is one money mistake I have made that, if I talked about it, might save someone else from the same thing?
3. What is one financial conversation I have been avoiding that I could gently start this week?

PRINCIPLE 10

Keep a Winning Attitude

Your mindset matters as much as the math.
Progress beats perfection.

The topic of money is emotional. It can cause fights, anxiety about the future, shame about past mistakes, and pressure to look successful even when you are struggling. A winning attitude does not mean ignoring any of that; it means choosing to believe that you can learn, grow, and get better at handling money, no matter where you start.

The Long Game

A music educator friend of mine once said something to his students that has stayed with me. He told them, "Most people overestimate what they can do in a week, and underestimate what they can do in a year." You could see the words land; a few students sat a little straighter, and the room got quiet in the way rooms do when something actually sinks in.

We live in a world that pushes for quick results, quick money, quick success, quick everything. It is easy to start a project with real energy, but then lose momentum just as fast when the results are not fast. A winning attitude is built differently; it shows up even when nothing feels exciting, keeps going when no one is watching, and understands somewhere beneath the surface that small steps repeated over time actually lead somewhere.

I have seen this play out again and again in music, in the classroom, and in life. The students who grow the most are rarely the most naturally talented; they are the ones who stick with it, make minor improvements, and come back the next day willing to try again. The same idea applies to money. Saving a small amount may not feel like much in the moment, and making one careful decision may not seem important on its own, but over time, those choices build on each other in ways that are hard to see until suddenly they are impossible to miss.

A winning attitude is not loud, and it does not need an audience. It is steady, it is patient, and it holds onto the belief that what you do consistently matters far more than what you do once in a while. That is how progress happens. That is the long game.

Five Mental Shifts That Change Everything

Shift #1: From "I Can't" to "I'm Learning." "I can't" is permanent. "I'm learning" is progress. Add the word "yet" to any limiting belief.

Shift #2: From Comparison to Your Own Path. You don't know a person's debt, their family situation, or their full story. Some people genuinely have more help, and that's real. Your only competition is yesterday's version of you.

Shift #3: From Shame to Data. Your bank balance is just data. Your debt is only a number with a plan. Shame keeps you stuck. Data helps you move forward.

Shift #4: From Perfection to Progress. Perfectionism quits. Progress keeps going. "I saved $50 this month. That's 50 more than zero."

Shift #5: From "Someday" to "Today." "Someday" never comes. Today is the only day you control.

Maya (Courage) reminds you: "I don't need to wait for perfect. I can start now, and I can keep going."

A winning attitude doesn't mean you never doubt yourself or never have a hard month. It means you keep going anyway, missing a savings goal and starting again instead of quitting, treating setbacks as data rather than verdicts, and trusting that steady effort adds up even when you can't see it yet.

The people who build real financial security aren't the ones who have never struggled. They're the ones who stayed in the game long enough for consistency to do its work.

SMALL STEP #10 – KEEP A WINNING ATTITUDE

Do This This Week:

- Write down three money wins from the past month, even small ones.
- Identify one limiting belief about money, and reframe it with the word "yet."
- Share one thing you've learned in this book with someone.

My three money wins:

1. ____

2. ____

3. ____

Old belief: I ______________________________.

New belief: I ______________________________**yet.**

Your Turn: Reflection Questions

1. What's one limiting belief I have about money?
2. What's one small money win I've had recently that I didn't celebrate?
3. What would change if I believed I could actually do this?

All of the Start Smart Crew members remind you: "We're all figuring this out together. You're not alone."

Sofia (Belief) reminds you: "You're doing fine. Keep going."

A Note Before You Move On

You now have 10 principles, not as rules to follow perfectly, but as tools to return to again and again. Some will feel immediately useful. Others will make more sense six months from now. That's exactly how it's supposed to work.

You've now worked through 10 principles. That matters. The wheel keeps turning. Keep going.

Interlude: Every Dollar You Earn Follows a Path

By now, you have seen 10 principles that can change the way you think about money, how small habits grow, why starting early matters, and how simplicity, awareness, and good decisions can make life easier down the road.

A very practical question usually comes next: "Okay, but what do I actually do with my money?"

Every dollar you earn follows a path, and that path is exactly what this section has been building toward. It begins with a paycheck, and before you ever see that money, taxes and other deductions have already been taken out. What remains is your net pay, the amount that actually lands in your account.

From there, the most important step begins. You make a plan for how that money is spent. Take a look at the Start Smart Money Flow illustration. That flow is exactly what we are talking about.

Once you have a plan, your money moves in four directions: (1) You save some, (2) spend some, (3) invest some, and (4) protect what you have built.

Those four choices quietly shape your financial life more than most people realize. Every day, millions of people earn money without ever stopping to think about where it is actually going, and that is exactly where this book has been trying to help. Understanding the path is where everything changes.

In the next section of this book, we're going to open the Start Smart Toolkit. Inside that toolkit are simple tools that help you guide your money along that path with confidence. Nothing complicated. Nothing is overwhelming. These are simply practical ideas that help you make steady progress, one smart decision at a time.

Let's get started.

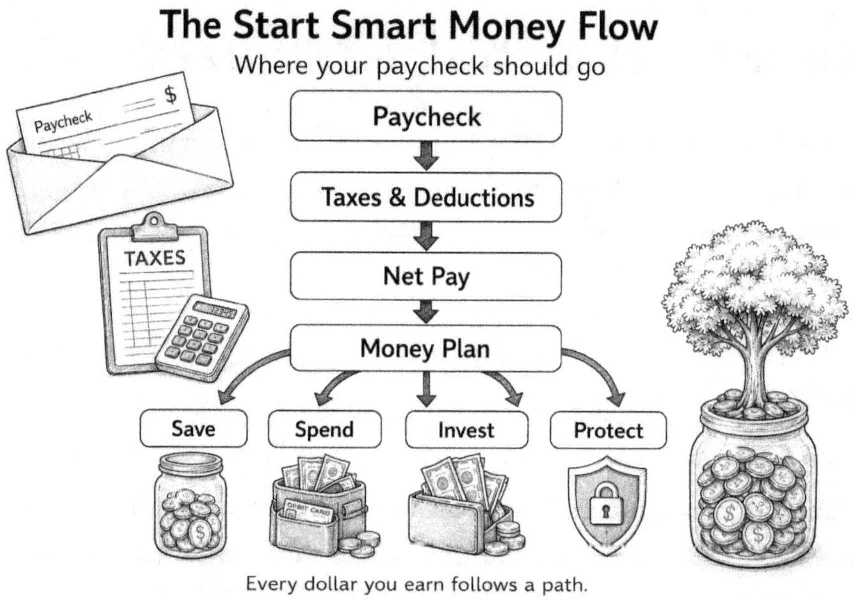

Every dollar you earn follows a path.
Smart money decisions start by understanding that path.

PART 4

Real-Life Money Toolkit

Practical Tools for the Moments That Matter

Start Here

You've built awareness, defined your vision, and learned the principles that help you make smart money decisions. Now comes the part where you put it all into practice: step-by-step how-to guides for the moments when you actually have to decide what to do with your money.

Part 4 is your reference section. Come back to it when you're opening your first bank account, reading a confusing paycheck, deciding whether to buy or lease a car, signing a lease, protecting yourself from scams, or figuring out student loans. It's also here for the bigger questions: what credit actually means, how insurance really works, and how to think about the career you're building.

You don't need to read this part straight through. Scan the section titles, find what matches your current situation, and use it as a guide.

Riley (Common Sense) reminds you: "Does this really make sense? These tools help you ask the right questions before you commit."

SECTION 1

Money Mistakes You Don't Have to Make

Small decisions with surprisingly big price tags

Every one of these mistakes has been made by a real student, and some by adults who should have known better. None of them are catastrophic, and nobody's life fell apart over a forgotten subscription or a bad Uber decision.

But all of them sting, and, more important, they're avoidable once you know what to look for.

The Free Trial Trap

You signed up for something "free" and forgot to cancel. It could be a study app, a streaming service you wanted for only one show, or that photo editing app you used once for a class project and never opened again.

Monthly charge: $9.99
Months before you noticed: 5
Total: $49.95

Takeaway: Free trials are only free if you remember them. Set a calendar reminder the moment you sign up, while it's still right in front of you.

The Overdraft Burrito

You swiped your card for an $8 meal, even though you had $7.50 in your account. Maybe you forgot about that other charge that hadn't posted yet, or maybe you just weren't paying attention.

Overdraft fee: $35
Cost of the burrito: $8
Total: $43

That's not a burrito anymore. It's a $43 lesson about keeping a buffer in your account.

Takeaway: Always leave a buffer in your checking account. Even $20 makes a difference, and it helps to check your balance before you swipe, not after.

The ATM That Isn't Yours

You grabbed $20 from a random ATM outside a concert venue or a convenience store because it was right there, and you needed cash.

Bank fee: $3
Machine fee: $4
Total cost to access your own money: $7

You paid $7 to access $20 of your own money. That math doesn't work in your favor.

Takeaway: Convenience almost always has a price. Sometimes it's worth paying, but most of the time it's not. Know the difference before you hit "Accept Fee."

The Ticket Surprise

You and a friend found tickets for $40 each, perfect and affordable. You click through to checkout and suddenly there's a service fee, a facility fee, a processing fee, and something called a "convenience fee," even though you're the one doing all the work to buy the ticket.

Two tickets at $40 each: $80
Final total after fees: $109

The first price is rarely the real price.

Takeaway: Never budget based on the advertised price. Always go all the way to the checkout screen before you decide if something is actually in your range.

The Cash App Typo

You sent $50 to the wrong username, one letter off. Maybe it autocorrected, maybe you were in a hurry, or maybe you simply misheard the name.

Money sent: $50
Money returned: $0

Unlike a bank, most payment apps treat this like handing cash to a stranger. Once it's gone, it's gone.

Takeaway: Check twice and send once. If it's a larger amount, send a $1 test first.

The Autopilot Subscription Drain

This one is different from forgetting a free trial. These are services you once used and paid for deliberately, then simply stopped needing.

Total monthly leakage: $30 to $50
Total yearly leakage: $360 to $600

Takeaway: If you never look at it, the amount doesn't stay small. It just grows without you noticing. Check your subscriptions every few months and cancel anything you're not actively using.

The Ride-Share Rainstorm

You skip the bus because it's raining, or you're running late, or you just don't feel like standing at the stop. Honestly, it makes sense.

Ride-share: $18
Bus: $2
Difference: $16

Takeaway: Convenience decisions add up quietly. They don't feel expensive in the moment, which is exactly what makes them easy to miss.

The Campus Parking Ticket

You "run in for a minute."

Meter: $1.50
Ticket: $40

Takeaway: Shortcuts often cost more than the long way.

SECTION 2

The Math That Actually Clicks

This section is not about cutting everything out. Nobody wants to live on rice and beans and never do anything fun. That's not the point.

The point is understanding what your habits are really costing you so you can decide what matters. Maybe the coffee is worth it to you. Great, keep the coffee. But at least know what you're trading for it.

The Lunch Swap

Pack lunch twice a week instead of buying.
Savings per week: about $30
Per year: about $1,080

What this adds up to: Two brown bags a week turns into over a thousand dollars by summer. That could be a real trip with friends, a solid chunk toward a used car, or simply a cushion you didn't have before.

The Coffee Creep

You started with plain coffee, then added oat milk, an extra shot, and a flavor syrup. Now your "simple coffee" is $6, and you get it three times a week.

Weekly: $18
Per year: about $540

Here's the part most people miss: "Once in a while" has a way of turning into a pattern, and patterns always come with a price tag.

The Summer Job Vanish

You worked hard all summer and made about $3,000, but without a plan you spent it on little things, gas, food, random Amazon orders, a few nights out, nothing that felt crazy at the time.

By October, you've spent about $1,440 of it, and you're not really sure what you spent it on.

What this comes down to: Money without a plan disappears. No matter how hard you worked for it, a simple note on your phone that says "Half of this goes to savings, the rest is for fun" makes all the difference.

The $100 Decision

You have $100. It's nothing life-changing, just a hundred bucks.

Option A: You spend it now on something fun and enjoy it for a few days or a few weeks before it fades into the background of your life.

Option B: You put it in an index fund and leave it alone, adding nothing else and letting it sit.

Over the next 40 years, that $100 could become around $2,000.

What this really means: Little money decisions today show up again years from now. You don't have to invest every dollar, but knowing what you're giving up by spending it now changes how some of those decisions feel.

The Convenience Tax

You already know about ATM fees and delivery markups. Here's the pattern underneath all of it: every time you pay for convenience, you're paying a tax on not planning ahead. The gas station drink instead of the water bottle you left at home. The delivery fee instead of the five-minute drive. The name brand instead of the identical generic sitting right next to it.

None of these are wrong choices every time. Sometimes convenience is genuinely worth it. But every one of them has a price, and that price is invisible until you add it up.

Convenience purchases three times a week: about $7 extra each time
Per year: over $1,000

This is not a lecture. It's just the math.

Your Turn

Here's the example that matters most, yours.

Think about the one habit in your own life that shows up on autopilot, the thing you spend on regularly without really deciding to. It might be food, it might be rides, it might be subscriptions you've stopped using, or something else entirely.

Write it down:

My habit: ______________________________

What it costs per week: $____

What it costs per year: $____

What I could do with that instead: ______________________________

You don't have to change it. But now you know what it costs, and knowing is the whole point of this section.

SECTION 3

Scripts for When the Pressure Is On

Sometimes the hardest part of managing money is not the math. The math itself is simple: spend less than you make, save something, and avoid bad debt.

The hard part is what to say when your friends are all spending money and you're trying not to; when someone offers to cover you and you know you'll forget to pay them back; or when someone calls you cheap because you're not doing what everyone else is doing.

Here are some things you can actually say, plain, normal sentences that work in real life.

When the group wants to go out to eat but you're trying to save:

"I'm into hanging out. I already ate. I'll grab something small."

What this does: You're not saying no to the social part, but you're opting out of the expensive part. Most people will not care what's on your plate.

When there's no plan at the mall, and you know you'll impulse buy if you wander around:

"I'm looking for one thing today."

What this does: It sets the boundary before you walk in and gives you an exit strategy. Once you find the thing, you leave.

When someone covers you and says "Get me back later":

"Send me the request now so I don't forget."

What this does: It makes you sound responsible, not cheap. You're not avoiding paying, you're making sure it actually happens.

When someone calls you cheap:

"I'm saving for something that matters to me."

What this does: It reframes the conversation. You're not cheap, you're focused, and there's a difference.

When everyone is upgrading to the more expensive version of something:

"I'm good with the original plan."

What this does: It's calm and neutral, and it doesn't invite argument. You're not judging their choice, just choosing not to match it.

When someone says "It's only money":

"I know. That's why I'm deciding where mine goes."

What this does: It's a gentle reminder that money is a tool, not a joke. You get to decide how to use yours.

When you feel the urge to buy something you didn't plan for:

"Do I actually want this, or do I really want the feeling of buying something right now?"

What this does: It forces a pause. The answer is often the second one, and knowing that is half the battle.

When someone asks you to split something unevenly:

“I’m happy to split evenly, but let’s make sure we’re all clear on the total first.”

What this does: It prevents the awkward moment later when someone feels shorted. Clarity now saves resentment later.

When you’re the one who always pays for the group, but gets paid back late:

“I can grab this one, but I’m going to send the request right now so I don’t have to chase anyone later.”

What this does: It’s friendly but firm. You’re doing the group a favor, and the least they can do is pay you back promptly.

When a friend asks to borrow money and you’re not sure they’ll pay it back:

“I’m not really in a position to lend money right now, but I’m happy to help you figure out another way to cover it.”

What this does: You’re not saying no to helping. You’re saying no to becoming a bank, and instead offering something real, your time and your thinking. If they’re a real friend, that’s actually more valuable.

When someone pressures you to go on a trip you can’t afford:

“That sounds amazing, but it’s not in the budget for me this time. Tag me in the photos though.”

What this does: You’re not saying that the trip is a bad idea or that you don’t want to go, you’re saying the money part doesn’t work right now, and leaving the door open for the next one.

When you're at a store and the salesperson is pushing the more expensive option:

"I appreciate it, but I'm going to stick with what I came in for."

What this does: It's polite and final, it doesn't invite further negotiation, and it reminds you why you walked in there in the first place.

When a group is splitting a bill and someone ordered way more than everyone else:

"I think it might be easier if we each pay for what we ordered. Happy to help do the math."

What this does: It addresses the awkwardness directly but kindly. You're not accusing anyone of anything. You're making sure no one quietly subsidizes someone else's expensive taste.

When your parents offer to pay for something, and you're not sure if you should let them:

"Are you sure? I can cover part of it if that helps."

What this does: It shows you're thinking about money, not just taking it. Parents notice that, and sometimes they'll still pay for the whole thing, but they'll respect you more for offering.

The 48-Hour Rule

You see something online that you want, not something you need. Put it in your cart or just keep it in your head, close the app, and walk away. If you still want it two days later and you have the money for it, then go ahead and decide. Most of the time you won't even remember it, and that's not a trick. It's your brain telling you the truth about what actually matters to you.

SECTION 4

Quick-Reference Cheat Sheets

This section is not for reading from beginning to end. It's for flipping to when you need a reminder, the kind of thing you screenshot and keep until the moment you need it.

If you remember nothing else, remember this:

- Spend from your net pay amount, not gross.
- If you cannot pay off a credit card this month, do not use it.
- Check subscriptions every three months.
- Never lend money you cannot afford to lose.
- Small purchases add up into big totals.
- Wait 48 hours before buying non-essentials.
- Generic brands are usually the same thing as name brands.
- Gift cards are real money. Use them within a month or give them to someone who will.

Understanding Your Paycheck

Gross Pay: What you earn before anything is taken out
Net Pay: What actually hits your bank account

Always budget from net pay. If you budget from gross pay, you're planning to spend money you will never have.

Credit Card Reality

If you pay your balance in full every month, credit cards are a useful tool. You build credit and maybe earn some rewards.

If you carry a balance, you pay interest, and it's always higher than you think. That $40 shirt becomes a $55 shirt faster than you realize.

The only winning move is to pay off the complete balance every month.

Emergency Fund

Goal: $500 in a separate savings account.

Use it for real needs:

- Flat tire
- Broken phone screen that prevents you from working or doing schoolwork
- Urgent care copay
- Emergency trip home

Do not use it for:

- Concert tickets
- A sale at your favorite store
- A weekend trip you "deserve"
- Help for a friend who overspent

Protect this money like it isn't yours to spend freely, because in a real emergency it's the only thing standing between you and a much bigger problem.

Index Fund, Simply

You don't need to be a stock market expert to invest in an index fun. Keep it simple is usually the best move.

Buying an index fund is like buying a tiny slice of hundreds of different companies at once. Instead of betting everything on one stock and hoping the value goes up, you spread your money across the whole economy.

Over long periods of time, the whole economy tends to grow, and that's really your bet. You buy the fund, leave it alone, and let time do the work.

The One-Minute Money Check

Once a week, open your banking app and look at:

- Your balance
- The last five transactions

That's it, one minute, which is less time than it takes to scroll through a single video.

By doing this regularly, you catch the weird charges early, remember what you actually spent, and stay aware of where your money is going. That awareness turns out to be most of the battle.

The "Can I Actually Afford This" Test

Before you buy something that's more than $20, ask yourself three questions:

- Do I have the cash for this right now, rather than using a credit card?
- If I buy this, what am I giving up later this week or this month?

- Will I still care about this thing in two weeks?

Two "yes" answers means maybe, three is a green light, and one or none means put it back.

When to Use a Credit Card vs. Debit Card

This distinction trips people up more than almost anything else, so here's the short version.

Debit card: Use for everyday stuff like coffee, gas, and groceries, things you can definitely pay for right now.

Credit card: Use for planned purchases you already have the money for and want the extra protection on, like online orders, hotel reservations, rental cars, or anything where you might need to dispute a charge.

Never: Change things you hope you'll have money for later. That's how the trouble starts.

So far, we've focused on the decisions you're making right now. What comes next is something you'll return to later, when life asks you bigger questions.

Tools For Right Now

The next section works differently from everything that has come before it. Rather than reading straight through, you'll come back to it when you need it. Find the tool that matches where you are right now, and use it as a guide.

You'll reach for some tools the week after graduation. You won't need others for a few years, but they'll be here when you do.

These are your go-to tools for real-life moments when you need a clear answer without a lot of background reading first. Opening a bank account, understanding your first paycheck, signing a lease, buying a car: each tool guides you in plain language.

Come back to these when a real decision comes up.

- **Tool 1:** Banking Basics—Opening Your Accounts
- **Tool 2:** Understanding Your Paycheck
- **Tool 3:** Your First Big Purchase—Transportation
- **Tool 4:** Renting 101
- **Tool 5:** Protecting Yourself—Scams and Fraud
- **Tool 6:** Credit Cards and Building Credit
- **Tool 7:** Student Loans: What You Need Before You Borrow
- **Tool 8:** Money Management Worksheets

Tools For What Comes Next

These tools go deeper into topics that can get more complicated once you're actually living with them, such as credit scores, insurance, student loans, taxes, and investing. Read them when you're ready to understand something more fully, or when a situation has grown beyond a quick answer.

You'll know when you need one of these.

- **Tool 9:** Credit Scores and Credit Reports
- **Tool 10:** Insurance Basics
- **Tool 11:** Student Loan Repayments, Options, and Long-Term Planning
- **Tool 12:** Career and Income Decisions
- **Tool 13:** Consumer Protection and Digital Money
- **Tool 14:** Taxes: What You Need to Know Before You File
- **Tool 15:** Investing Basics
- **Tool 16:** How to Make Better Financial Decisions

A note on the Start Smart Crew: You'll find them at the end of every tool in this section, as you did throughout the book. Each crew member represents a trait that you're building in yourself, and when you see their name, it's worth taking a moment to consider what they're really asking of you.

Find the tool that matches where you are right now, work through it, and come back whenever you need it.

Tools for Right Now

TOOL 1: Banking Basics—Opening Your Accounts

Step 1: Choose where to open your account

- **Credit unions:** usually lower fees, member-owned
- **Online banks:** strong apps, often higher interest
- **Traditional banks:** convenient if you like in-person service

Step 2: Bring these with you

- Photo ID (driver's license, passport, state ID)
- Social Security number
- \$25–\$100 to open (varies by institution)
- Proof of address (utility bill, lease, official mail)

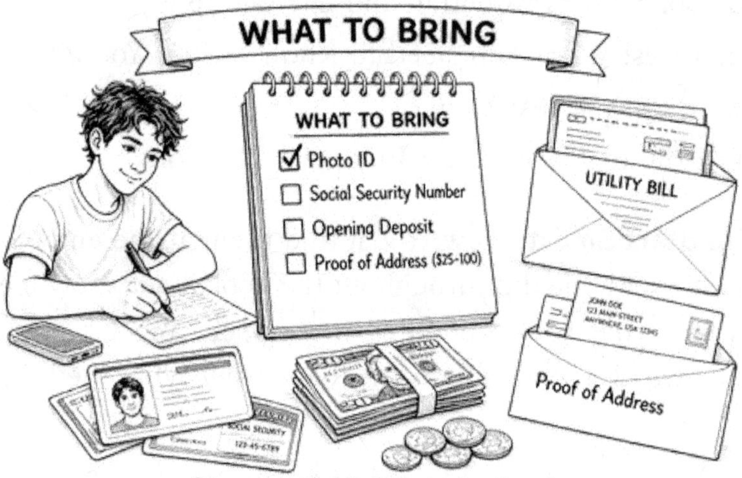

Same saving habit. Different growth engine.
Over time, the engine matters.

Step 3: Ask these questions before opening

- "What are the monthly maintenance fees?" (Aim for \$0.)
- "Is there a minimum balance requirement?"
- "How does overdraft protection work?"
- "Do you have a good mobile banking app?"

Savings Account Tips

Look for a higher-yield savings account with no monthly fees and no minimum balance, set up automatic transfers, and make this money harder to touch than your checking account.

Riley (Common Sense) reminds you: "What system can help make this easier on myself? Automation makes saving happen before I can spend it."

TOOL 2: Understanding Your Paycheck

Gross pay = what you earn on paper
Net pay = what actually hits your bank account

The difference results from taxes and deductions:

- Federal income tax
- State income tax (in most states)
- Social Security (around 6.2%)
- Medicare (around 1.45%)
- Health insurance (if offered)
- Retirement contributions (if enrolled)

KEY INSIGHT: If you don't understand your paycheck, ask your HR department. Understanding your paycheck is smart, not shameful.

TOOL 3: Your First Big Purchase—Transportation

KEY INSIGHT: A car is transportation, not a status symbol.

Most people think about the monthly payment only when they're looking at a car. That's a mistake, and it's one of the most common ones people make when they're starting out.

The Real Costs of Owning a Car

Expense	Monthly Cost
Monthly payment (if financed)	\$200–\$500+
Insurance	\$100–\$300
Gas	\$100–\$200
Maintenance	\$50–\$100 (averaged)
Repairs	\$0–\$500 (unpredictable)
Registration/taxes	\$50–\$100 (annual, divided by 12)
TOTAL	\$500–\$1,750 / month

That \$300/month car payment? It's really a \$700/month payment once you add everything else in.

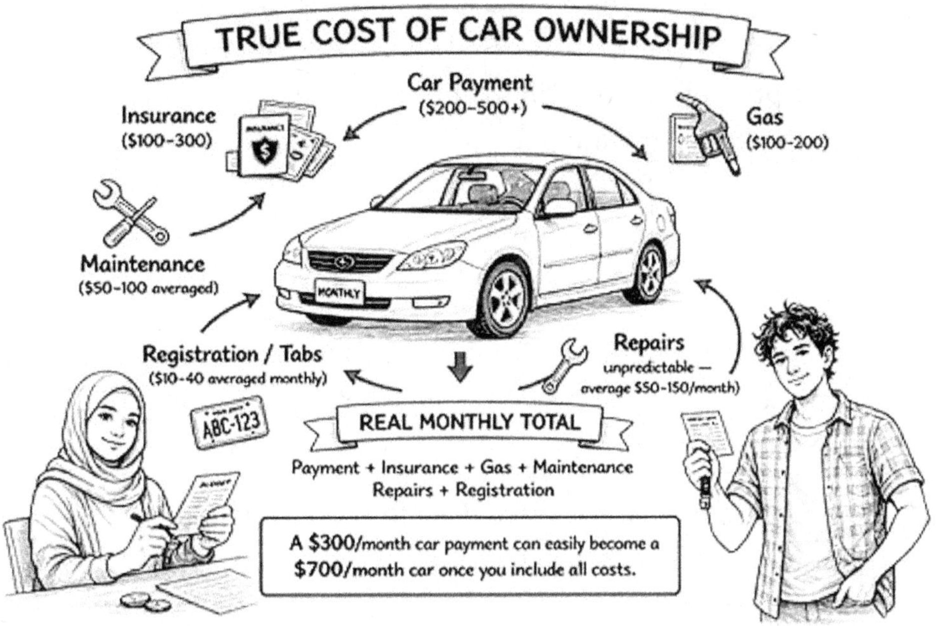

New vs. Used: What the Numbers Actually Show

Buying a new car means a $30,000 purchase price that loses 20% of its value the moment you drive off the lot. That is $6,000 gone instantly. Over the first five years, depreciation reaches about 60%, or $18,000. **Total five-year cost:** around $45,000 or more.

Buying a used car, say a car that's three years old, means a $15,000 purchase price on a vehicle that has already absorbed the worst of the depreciation and still has five to ten years of life left in it. **Total five-year cost:** around $25,000.

The difference is more than $20,000, and that's not being cheap. That's being smart about where your money goes.

Smart Car Buying Rules

- If the payment scares you, the car is too expensive.
- Consider a certified pre-owned car, which is essentially a used car that comes with a warranty.
- Pay cash if possible, even if it means buying a less expensive car

- Never finance longer than four years. If you need a longer loan to make the payment work, you can't actually afford the car.
- Get pre-approved for a loan before you start shopping.
- Budget for the total cost, not just the payment: insurance, gas, and maintenance all count.

When It Makes Sense to Buy vs. Use Alternatives

Buying a car is the right call for some people and the wrong call for others, and the difference usually comes down to where you live and what you actually need.

Buy a car when you live somewhere with no reliable public transit, you need it for work, you've saved at least $2,000 for unexpected repairs, and you can afford the total monthly cost without stretching your budget.

Consider alternatives when you live in a city with good public transit, you can bike or walk to most places, you need a car only occasionally, or buying one right now would drain your emergency fund.

A car is a tool. Buy the tool when you need it and can afford the whole cost of it, not just the sticker price.

Riley (Common Sense) reminds you: "Does this actually make sense for my situation? Total cost, not just the monthly payment, is the number that matters."

TOOL 4: Renting 101

Signing a lease is probably the biggest financial commitment you'll make before you buy a car or take on a student loan. Most people read the lease too fast, miss the things that matter, and end up paying for it later, sometimes literally.

Here's what to know before you sign anything.

The Real Cost of Renting

Total monthly housing cost includes more than rent:

- Rent
- Renters insurance
- Utilities (electric, gas, water, ask which are included)
- Internet
- Parking (if not included)
- Laundry (if not in-unit)

A place advertising $900 a month can easily cost $1,150 once you add everything in. Always ask what's included and what isn't before you fall in love with the apartment.

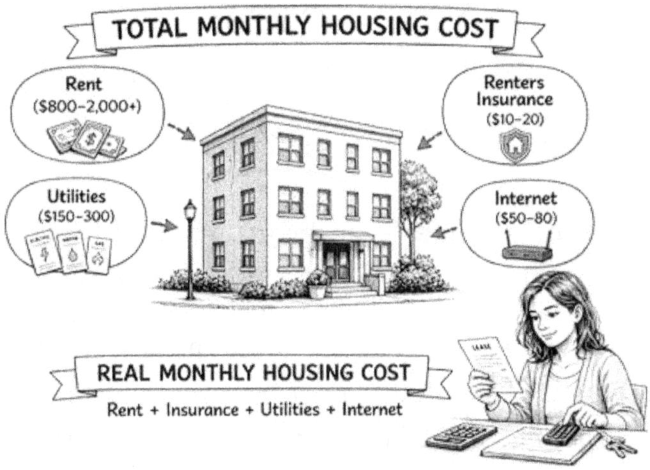

Before You Sign: Questions to Ask

These are not optional questions. If a landlord gets annoyed that you're asking them, that tells you something important.

- What is the monthly rent, and when is it due?
- What utilities are included?
- How much is the security deposit, and what are the conditions for getting it back?

- What is the lease term, month-to-month, six months, one year?
- Does the lease automatically renew? If so, how much notice do you need to give before moving out?
- How does maintenance work? Who do you call, and how fast do they respond?
- Is there a penalty for breaking the lease early?
- Are pets allowed, and is there an additional deposit?

That question about early termination matters more than people think. Life changes, jobs move, roommates fall through, circumstances shift. Knowing what it will costs to get out before you're locked in is worth asking on day one.

The Security Deposit: Protect Yourself

Your security deposit is typically one to two months of rent, held by the landlord and returned when you move out, minus any damages they can document.

The problem is that "damages" can be interpreted broadly, and some landlords keep deposits they shouldn't. Here's how you protect yourself:

On move-in day, before you unpack a single box, walk through the entire apartment and document everything. Take photos and short videos of every room, every wall, every appliance, every scuff, scratch, and stain that is already there. Send those photos to your landlord in writing, a text or email, so there is a timestamp and a record. Do the same thing on move-out day.

This one step, which takes about 15 minutes, has saved people hundreds of dollars.

Roommates: Get It in Writing

Splitting rent with someone is a financial arrangement, not just a living situation. Even if the other person is your best friend, clarify these things before move-in:

- Who is on the lease?
- How is the rent split, and who sends the payment to the landlord?
- How are utilities divided?
- What happens if one person wants to leave early?
- What are the ground rules for shared spaces, guests, and noise?

If only one person's name is on the lease, that person is legally responsible for the full rent, even if the roommate stops paying. Understand that before you agree to it.

Read the Lease Before You Sign It

A lease is a legal document. It is binding the moment you sign it. That means you need to read it, all of it, not just skim it while the landlord is standing there waiting.

Things to look for:

Automatic renewal clause: Some leases renew automatically for another full term unless you give written notice 30 to 60 days before the end date. Miss that window and you may be locked in for another year.

Early termination penalty: The penalty is usually one to two months of rent. Know the number before you need it.

What counts as a lease violation: Subletting, pets, or having a long-term guest can all be grounds for eviction in some leases.

Rent increase terms: Some leases specify how much rent can go up at renewal. Others don't. Ask.

If something in the lease is unclear, ask the landlord to explain it in writing. If they won't, or can't, that's a red flag.

Renters Insurance: GET IT

This insurance costs very little per month. It protects your stuff if it's stolen or damaged, and it covers liability if someone gets hurt in your apartment. Your landlord's insurance covers the building. It does not cover your laptop, your clothes, or anything else that belongs to you.

A cheap renters policy covers thousands of dollars in personal property for a few dollars a month. It's the easiest financial protection you can buy, and most people skip it until they wish they hadn't.

Riley (Common Sense) reminds you: "Does this actually make sense? Read the lease once for the big picture, then read it again looking for the things that could cost you money later."

TOOL 5: Protecting Yourself—Scams and Fraud

NEVER give these out unless you initiated the contact:

- Social Security number
- Bank account passwords or login credentials
- Credit card CVV code
- One-time security codes sent to your phone
- PIN numbers

Red Flags—Signs of a Scam

- **Urgency:** "Act now or lose this opportunity!"
- **Too good to be true:** "Make thousands a week from home!"

- **Requests for payment via gift cards**, wire transfer, or cryptocurrency.
- **Unsolicited contact:** someone called, emailed, or texted you first.
- **Threats:** "Your account will be closed" or "You'll be arrested."

Common Scams That Target Young Adults

Phishing emails and texts

You get a text that looks exactly like it's from your bank. Same logo, same font, same tone. It says your account has been locked and gives you a link to verify your information. You click on the link, enter your login, and hand your credentials directly to a stranger.

What to do: Don't click on links in texts or emails, even if they look real. Close the message, open a new browser tab, and go directly to your bank's website. The real bank will be there. The fake one won't.

Fake job offers

You see a posting online: flexible hours, work from home, great pay, no experience needed. You apply and hear back within the hour. They want to hire you immediately, no interview, and they ask for your Social Security number and bank account information to set up direct deposit.

What to do: Research the company independently before you give anyone anything. A real employer will have a real website, real reviews, and a real hiring process. Never pay money to get a job, and never hand over personal information before you've verified who you're actually talking to.

IRS impersonators

You get a call from someone claiming to be from the IRS. They say you owe back taxes and if you don't pay immediately, you'll be arrested.

They want payment by gift card or wire transfer right now, before you hang up.

What to do: Hang up. The IRS does not call you out of nowhere, does not threaten arrest, and does not ask for gift cards. Ever. If you're genuinely worried you owe taxes, go directly to irs.gov yourself and check.

Romance scams

Someone finds you online, starts a conversation, and over days or weeks becomes someone you feel like you know. They're kind, they're consistent, and they seem genuinely interested in you. Then something comes up; an emergency, a plane ticket, a situation only you can help with, and they need money.

What to do: Never send money to someone you haven't met in person, no matter how real the relationship feels. This particular scam works precisely because it doesn't feel like a scam.

Check overpayment scams

Someone sends you a check for more than they owe you, for a sold item, a gig job, or something similar, and asks you to deposit it and send back the difference. The check looks real. Your bank may even show it as deposited. But when it bounces days later, the money you sent back is already gone and the loss is yours.

What to do: Never deposit checks from people you don't know, and never send money back to someone who overpaid you. A legitimate buyer or employer does not make that kind of mistake.

Coach Rule

If something feels weird, slow down and think it through. You don't owe anyone an immediate answer. You don't owe anyone your personal information. When in doubt, verify.

If You've Been Scammed, Act Immediately

- Call your bank/credit card company
- Change all passwords
- Put a "credit freeze" on your accounts with the three credit bureaus (Equifax, Experian, and TransUnion). This stops anyone from opening new credit in your name until you unfreeze it.
- File a report with the appropriate consumer protection agency

TOOL 6: Credit Cards and Building Credit

A credit card in the right hands is a useful tool. In the wrong hands, or without the right information, it's one of the fastest ways to sink your finances before they've had a chance to get started.

Most young adults are never taught how credit cards actually work before they get one. That's not your fault. But once you have one, here's what you need to know.

How Credit Cards Actually Work

When you use a credit card, you're borrowing money from the card issuer. Every month, you receive a statement showing what you owe. If you pay the full balance by the due date, you pay zero interest and your credit score benefits.

If you carry a balance, interest starts building. Many cards charge high annual interest rates. Carrying a $1,000 balance and making only minimum payments can cost you hundreds in interest and take years to pay off.

That's the minimum payment trap. It's common, costly, and completely avoidable once you understand how it works.

The One Rule That Changes Everything

> **KEY INSIGHT:** *Pay your full balance every month whenever possible. When you pay in full, you pay zero interest, build your credit score, and use the card exactly the way it's designed to benefit you.*

If paying in full isn't possible right now, pay as much above the minimum as you can, and do it as fast as possible. Every extra dollar reduces the interest building against you. And pause new charges until the balance is gone.

One more thing worth saying plainly: a credit card is not extra money. It's a payment tool. Avoid using it to buy things you couldn't afford with cash.

Understanding Your Credit Card Statement

- Statement balance: the total you owed at the end of the billing cycle.
- Minimum payment: the smallest amount the issuer will accept.
- Payment due date: when payment must arrive to avoid late fees and hits to your score.
- APR (annual percentage rate): your yearly interest rate on carried balances.
- Available credit: how much credit remains unused. Lower balances relative to your limit help your score.

What to Look for in Your First Card

- No annual fee
- Modest starting limit
- Simple rewards (if any)
- From a bank or credit union you trust

If you're building or rebuilding credit, a secured card, backed by a small deposit, can be a safe start.

Credit Cards and Your Credit Score

Key factors:

- Payment history (on-time or not)
- Credit utilization (how much of your limit you use)
- Length of history
- Mix of accounts
- New credit opened

Paying on time and keeping balances low relative to your limit are two of the biggest levers you control.

If you're already in credit card debt, remember: you're not alone, and this is fixable. The most important steps are to stop growing the balance, choose a repayment strategy (highest interest first or smallest balance first), and keep going.

TOOL 7: Student Loans: What You Need Before You Borrow

Student loans may be the biggest financial commitment you've ever made, and most people sign the paperwork without fully understanding what they agreed to.

First, Know What You Owe

> **KEY INSIGHT:** *This is the part where you stop guessing and actually look at the real numbers.*

Before you can make smart decisions, you need a clear picture. Log in to the official federal student aid website to see every federal loan you have, who services it, the interest rate, and your current balance. If you have private loans, check with your lender directly. Write it all down.

What you're looking for:

- Total balance on each loan
- Interest rate for each loan
- Loan servicer (who you pay)
- Whether each loan is federal or private

Federal and private loans work differently. Federal loans have more protections and repayment options. Private loans have fewer. Know which you have.

Understand How Interest Works

Capitalization happens when unpaid interest gets added to your principal balance, so you end up owing interest on your interest. Understanding this early can save you money.

Your Repayment Options (Federal Loans)

Standard Repayment: Payments are fixed for about 10 years. This plan pays off your loan the fastest and costs you the least in total interest, if you can afford the payment.

Income-Driven Repayment (IDR): Your payment is based on what you actually earn, not just what you owe. This is the option that matters most for a lot of new graduates. Here's what that looks like in real life: on a $35,000 salary, a standard repayment plan might run around $300 a month. An income-driven plan on that same salary might run closer to $90. Same loan, but very different monthly number. If money is tight in your first few years out of school, this option can keep you from falling behind while you get established.

Graduated Repayment: Payments start lower and increase over time. This can work if you're confident your income will grow, but you'll pay more in total interest than on the standard plan.

Public Service Loan Forgiveness (PSLF): If you work for a qualifying employer, such as a government agency or nonprofit, you may be eligible for forgiveness after a set number of qualifying payments. The rules are specific and have changed over the years, so read carefully and verify current requirements before you count on it.

Riley (Common Sense) reminds you: "Does this actually make sense for my situation? The right plan isn't the most common plan, it's the one that fits my real life."

What to Do Right Now

- Log in to your federal loan portal and find your loan details.
- Write down every loan: balance, interest rate, and servicer.
- Confirm your repayment plan; research whether if another plan fits better.
- Set up autopay (many servicers offer a small rate reduction).
- If you're struggling, contact your servicer before you miss a payment.

Student loan debt is real, and it can feel heavy. But it's manageable with a plan. Ignoring it makes it worse. Knowing your numbers, choosing the right repayment option, and making consistent payments protect your credit and keep you moving forward.

TOOL 8: Money Management Worksheets

Monthly Budget Worksheet (50/30/20 Framework)

You met this framework in Principle 6. Here's where you fill it in with your own numbers. Use your monthly take-home pay (after taxes) as your starting point.

The Three Categories

Needs (around 50%): housing, utilities, groceries, transportation, minimum loan payments, health insurance

Wants (around 30%): dining out, streaming, entertainment, clothing beyond basics, hobbies

Savings and Debt Payoff (around 20%): emergency fund, Pay Yourself First transfer, extra debt payments, retirement contributions

50/30/20 Budget Worksheet

My monthly take-home pay (after taxes): $

NEEDS (50% = $____)

Rent/mortgage: $____

Utilities: $____

Groceries: $____

Transportation: $____

Minimum loan payments: $____

Health insurance: $____

Other: $____

WANTS (30% = $____)

Dining out: $____

Streaming and subscriptions: $____

Entertainment: $____

Clothing (beyond basics): $____

Hobbies: $____

Other: $____

SAVINGS AND DEBT PAYOFF (20% = $____)

Emergency fund contribution: $____

Pay Yourself First transfer: $____

Extra debt payments: $____

Retirement contribution: $____

If your needs exceed 50%, that's okay, especially early in your career. The framework is a guide, not a rule. Use it to see your spending clearly, not to judge it.

Net Worth Tracker (update every 6–12 months)

ASSETS (What You Own)

Checking account(s): $____

Savings account(s): $____

Retirement accounts: $____

Investment accounts: $____

Vehicle value: $____

Other: $____

TOTAL ASSETS: $____

LIABILITIES (What You Owe)

Credit card balances: $____

Student loans: $____

Car loan: $____

Other loans: $____

Other: $____

TOTAL LIABILITIES: $____

NET WORTH = TOTAL ASSETS – TOTAL LIABILITIES = $____

Goal: *watch this number move in the right direction over time. Even if it starts negative, which is common, progress is what matters.*

A Note on Apps

The worksheet is here for a reason. Working through the numbers yourself, even once, helps you understand what the categories mean and where your money actually goes. But you don't have to track everything by hand to make this work. Most banks now have budget tools built right into their app, already connected to your account and free to use.

If you want a more dedicated app, here are some worth looking at.

YNAB (You Need a Budget) is thorough and well-respected, especially if you want to give every dollar a job. **Copilot** is popular with younger users who want something cleaner and easier to look at. **PocketGuard** is simple and good for students who just want to know how much is safe to spend right now. **Goodbudget** uses a digital envelope system, which works well if you liked the way this book thinks about categories. **EveryDollar** is straightforward and free to start. **Cleo** is worth mentioning because it connects to your accounts and talks to you in plain language, which some people find easier to actually engage with.

Pick a tool that feels simple enough that you'll actually use it. A budget app you actually open is worth ten that you download and forgot about.

You have what you need. Use it the next time money decisions come up.

Tools For What Comes Next

Looking for something specific? Here's where to go in this section:

- **Credit and Debt Help**—Tools 9, 11
- **Insurance and Protection**—Tool 10 (see also Tool 5 in the earlier section)
- **Career and Income**—Tool 12
- **Consumer Protection and Digital Money**—Tool 13
- **Taxes and Investing**—Tools 14, 15
- **Better Decisions**—Tool 16

TOOL 9: Credit Scores and Credit Reports

Most people hear the words "credit score" and feel a vague sense of anxiety. Maybe they're not exactly sure what it is, or maybe they've already made a credit mistake and aren't sure how bad the damage is.

Here's the good news: a credit score is not a mystery, and it's not a judgment of your worth as a person. It's a number that reflects one specific thing, namely how reliably you've repaid borrowed money. Once you understand how a credit score works, you can control it.

What Is a Credit Score?

A credit score is a three-digit number, typically between 300 and 850, that lenders use to decide whether to lend you money and at what interest rate. The higher the score, the less risky you appear to a lender.

Your score comes from your credit report, which is a detailed history of every time you've borrowed money: credit cards, student loans, car loans, and even some utility accounts. The three main credit bureaus, Equifax, Experian, and TransUnion, collect that information and use it to generate your score.

What the Numbers Mean

- **750 and above:** *Excellent*—you'll likely qualify for the best rates
- **700–749:** *Very good*—strong approval odds, competitive rates
- **650–699:** *Good*—you'll qualify for most things, though rates may be higher
- **600–649:** *Fair*—some lenders will approve you, but terms may not be great
- **Below 600:** *Building needed*—limited options, higher rates, or denied

These ranges aren't permanent, and a score can move up or down within months depending on your habits. Wherever you are right now isn't where you have to stay.

What Affects Your Score

The five main factors, roughly in order of importance:

- **Payment history (around 35%):** Whether you pay on time. This is the biggest factor by far. While one late payment won't destroy your score, a pattern of late payments will.
- **Credit utilization (around 30%):** How much of your available credit you're using. If your credit limit is $1,000 and you're carrying an $800 balance, your utilization is 80%, which is high. Most advisors suggest keeping it below 30%.
- **Length of credit history (around 15%):** How long your accounts have been open. This is why keeping an old card open, even one you rarely use, can help your score.
- **Credit mix (around 10%):** Whether you have different types of credit, such as a credit card and a student loan. You don't need to take on new debt just to improve this factor.
- **New credit (around 10%):** How recently you've applied for credit. Each application triggers a hard inquiry that temporarily lowers your score by a few points.

Hard Inquiries: What They Are and When They Matter

When you apply for a credit card, car loan, apartment, or any other credit product, the lender pulls your credit report, which counts as a hard inquiry. It signals to credit bureaus that you're seeking new credit and temporarily lowers your score, usually by five to ten points. One or two hard inquiries are no big deal, but applying for several credit cards in a short period adds up and can meaningfully lower your score. Space out applications and apply only when you actually need the product.

The Minimum Payment Trap

If you carry a balance, the minimum payment is designed to keep you in debt, not to get you out of it. The credit card section of this book explains exactly how this works and what it costs you over time. The short version: pay as much above the minimum as you can every month, and stop adding to the balance while you do it.

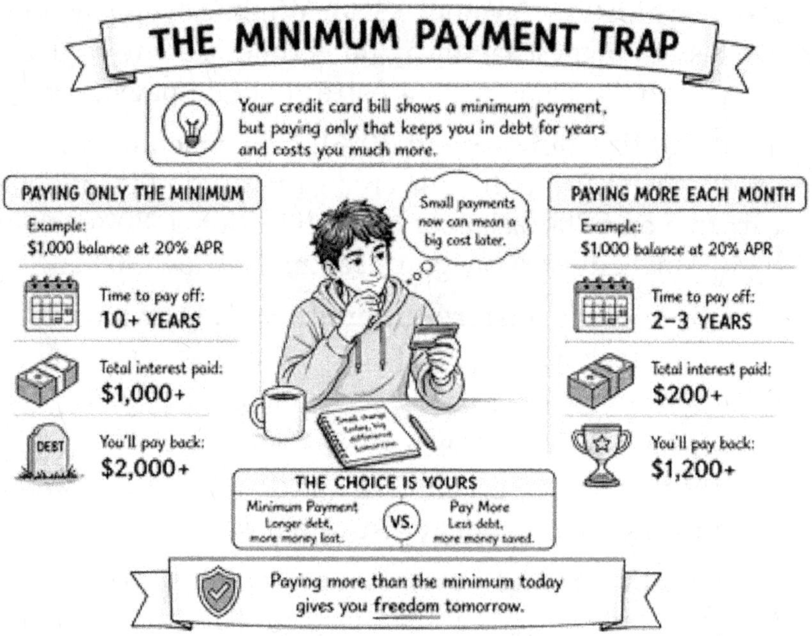

Co-Signing: Understand What You're Agreeing To

If a friend or family member asks you to co-sign a loan, you're not just vouching for them. You're legally responsible for the debt if they don't pay, and every missed payment appears on your credit report, even though you didn't make the purchase. If your friend defaults, the lender can come after you. Co-signing isn't always a bad choice, but it's a serious one. Do it only if you genuinely trust the person and could afford to make the payments yourself if necessary.

How to Check Your Credit Report Safely

You're entitled to one free credit report from each bureau every year. The official, government-authorized site is AnnualCreditReport.com. Be cautious of other sites that offer "free" reports, as many try to sign you up for a paid monitoring service. When you pull your report, review it carefully for accounts that aren't yours, incorrect balances or payment histories, and any accounts you don't recognize. If something looks wrong, you have the right to dispute it, and errors do get corrected.

Identity Theft: The Basics

Identity theft occurs when someone uses your personal information, such as your name, Social Security number, date of birth, or financial account details, to open accounts, take out loans, or make purchases in your name. Young adults are frequently targeted because they often have clean credit histories and may not check their reports regularly. By the time someone notices, the damage can be significant.

Signs something might be wrong:

- You receive bills or collection notices for accounts you didn't open
- Your credit score drops unexpectedly
- You're denied credit for something that should have been easy to obtain

Unfamiliar accounts appear on your credit report. If you suspect identity theft, place a fraud alert or credit freeze with the three bureaus and report it to the FTC at identitytheft.gov. A credit freeze prevents new accounts from being opened in your name until you lift it.

Common Young Adult Credit Mistakes

- Missing a payment because you forgot, not because you couldn't afford it. Set up autopay for at least the minimum payment so this never happens.
- Maxing out a card, even if you pay it off monthly, because high utilization still affects your score mid-cycle.
- Closing old cards you're not using, which can shorten your credit history and raise your utilization ratio.
- Opening several new cards at once for rewards.
- Ignoring your credit report until something goes wrong.

KEY INSIGHT: *Your credit score isn't fixed, and it's not a grade on your life. It's a tool that responds to your behavior. Consistently applying good habits will improve it over time.*

SMALL STEP: *Pull your credit report this week at AnnualCreditReport.com. You don't need to do anything with it right now. Just review it and understand what's there.*

Lucas (Responsibility) reminds you: "My credit score is a reflection of my habits, not a grade on my worth. I can control this."

TOOL 10: Insurance Basics

Insurance is one of those topics that feels boring until the moment you need it. When it suddenly feels like the most important thing in the world. The goal of this section is simple: help you understand enough so you're not blindsided by the bill when something goes wrong.

Here's why insurance exists: life is unpredictable, and cars crash, apartments flood, and people get sick in ways no one plans for. Insurance pools risk, with many people paying a small amount regularly so that when something bad happens to one of them, the cost doesn't have to come entirely from that person's pocket.

You probably won't use your insurance most months, and that's fine because that's actually the point. The month you do need it is the month you'll be very glad it exists.

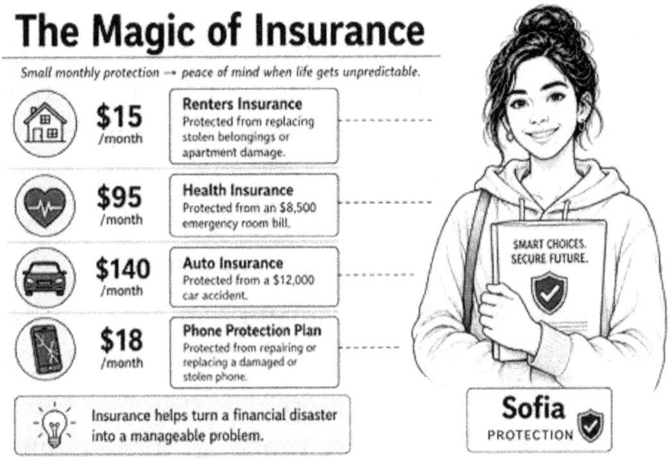

The Words You Need to Know

Premium: The amount you pay regularly, usually monthly, to keep your insurance active. Think of it as the cost of coverage, whether or not you ever use it.

Deductible: The amount you pay out of pocket before your insurance pays. If your car insurance has a $500 deductible and you get in a fender bender that costs $1,200 to fix, you pay the first $500 and your insurance covers the rest.

Co-pay: A flat fee you pay at the time of a medical visit. You might pay a $25 co-pay to see your doctor, and your insurance covers the rest.

Coverage limit: The maximum amount your insurance will pay. Anything above that limit is your responsibility.

Liability: Coverage for damage or injury you cause to other people or their property.

Auto Insurance: What You're Actually Paying For

If you drive a car, auto insurance isn't optional because it's required by law in every state. Most people don't fully understand what they're buying. Here's what's actually in a typical policy:

- **Liability coverage:** Pays for damage you cause to other people or their cars. This is the part the law requires, and if you rear-end someone, it covers their repairs and medical bills up to your policy limit.
- **Collision coverage:** Pays to fix or replace your own car after an accident, regardless of who was at fault.
- **Comprehensive coverage:** Covers non-collision damage, such as theft, a tree falling on your car, hail, or a deer strike.
- **Uninsured/underinsured motorist:** Protects you if you're hit by someone who has no insurance or not enough to cover your costs.

Real-life scenario: Jordan is 19 and just got his license. He has an older car worth about $4,000 and is deciding whether to carry full coverage or just liability. Full coverage would cost about $150 a month, while liability-only would cost about $60 a month. With full coverage, if he totals his car, he would receive a payout, but with liability-only, if he totals his car in an at-fault accident, he would receive nothing and would still need to find a way to replace it. The question isn't which is cheaper per month, but whether he has the savings to absorb the loss if the car becomes undrivable.

Health Insurance: The Parts That Confuse People

If you're under 26, you can usually stay on a parent's health insurance plan, which is often the simplest option if it's available. But once you're off their plan, or if they don't have one, you'll need to get your own.

Health insurance has a specific vocabulary that trips people up:

- **In-network vs. out-of-network:** Your insurance has agreements with certain doctors and hospitals. If you see someone outside that network, you usually pay significantly more.
- **Premium:** What you pay every month for the plan, whether or not you use it.
- **Deductible:** What you pay before insurance covers most costs. A plan with a $2,000 deductible means you pay the first $2,000 of medical bills yourself each year.
- **Out-of-pocket maximum:** The most you can be required to pay in a year. After you hit this limit, insurance covers 100% of covered costs for the rest of the year.

Real-life scenario: Noor is 22 and has no health insurance because she felt healthy and thought the premiums were expensive. In November, she broke her wrist while hiking, and the emergency room visit cost $8,500. Without insurance, that bill was entirely hers. With even a basic insurance plan at $120 a month, she would have paid her deductible and co-pays, probably about $1,500 total, and insurance would have covered the rest. The thing about health insurance is that you don't know when you'll need it, and when you do, the bills are rarely small.

Renters Insurance: The Easiest Call You'll Make

Renters insurance is one of the least expensive and most overlooked types of insurance for young adults, typically costing between $10 and $25 a month. It covers three main things:

- **Personal property:** If your belongings are stolen, damaged in a fire, or destroyed by a covered event, renters insurance reimburses you.

- **Liability:** If a guest slips and falls in your apartment and decides to sue, insurance covers legal costs and damages.
- **Additional living expenses:** If your apartment becomes uninhabitable due to a fire or flood, renters insurance often covers your temporary housing costs while repairs happen.

Real-life scenario: Sofia and two roommates came home after spring break to find that their apartment had been broken into. A laptop, a gaming console, some cash, and a few other items were gone. Sofia had renters insurance, but her roommates didn't, so she filed a claim and recovered most of what was taken, while her roommates had to absorb the loss out of pocket right in the middle of the semester. Your landlord's insurance covers the building but nothing you own. Renters insurance is a few dollars a month for the peace of mind of knowing that your belongings are protected.

Life Insurance

Life insurance is one type of insurance you probably don't need right now, but it's worth knowing it exists. If you ever have people depending on your income, like a spouse or children, that's when it becomes a conversation worth having.

Why Young Adults Often Skip Insurance

The most common reason is simple: it feels like paying for something you'll never use, and most months that's true. Young people are generally healthy, they're careful drivers, and nothing catastrophic has happened to them yet, but the reason nothing catastrophic has happened yet isn't because it can't happen, it's because it hasn't. Insurance is for the day when your luck runs out, and you can't know when that day is or how expensive it will be. The cost of not having insurance, on the one occasion when you need it, is almost always more than what you'd have paid in premiums to have it.

KEY INSIGHT: *Insurance isn't about expecting the worst. It's about not being financially ruined when the unexpected happens. The small monthly payment is what makes a bad day survivable.*

SMALL STEP: *Look up the cost of renters insurance this month. Most policies take about 10 minutes to set up online and cost less than a streaming subscription.*

Sofia (Belief) reminds you: "I don't buy insurance because I expect the worst. I buy it because I believe my future is worth protecting."

TOOL 11: Student Loans: Repayment, Options, and Long-Term Planning

Student loans may be the biggest financial commitment you have ever made, and most people sign the paperwork without fully understanding what they are agreeing to. That is not a criticism. The process moves fast, the forms are dense, and no one hands you a plain-language explanation when you need it most, but once you have a student loan, the best thing you can do is stop avoiding the numbers and start understanding them.

So let's do that together.

First, Know What You Owe

The first step is simply knowing what you owe. Log in to studentaid.gov, the official federal student aid website, and look up every federal loan in your name, including the balance, interest rate, and the name of your servicer, the company that handles your payments. If you have private loans through a bank or lender, check with them directly and add those to the same list. Write it all down somewhere you can find it.

What you are looking for: the total balance on each loan, the interest rate, who you send payments to, and whether each loan is federal or private. That last one matters more than most people realize. Federal loans come with protections and repayment options that private loans typically do not offer, and knowing which kind you have shapes every decision that follows.

Understand How Interest Works

Once you know your numbers, the next thing to understand is how interest works. This is where many people get quietly hurt without realizing it. When you are not paying down the interest on a loan, that unpaid interest is eventually added to your principal balance. Now you owe interest on a larger balance than you originally borrowed. This is called capitalization, and understanding it early can save you a meaningful amount of money over the life of your loan.

Your Repayment Options

Most people do not realize there is more than one way to repay a federal student loan. Choosing the right plan for where you are now can make a real difference in your monthly budget, so it is worth understanding what is available before you default to whatever your servicer sets up automatically.

The standard repayment plan spreads fixed payments over about 10 years. If you can afford the payment, this is usually the fastest path to paying off your loan and the least expensive in total interest over time.

If the standard payment feels out of reach right away, you are not out of options. Income-driven repayment bases your monthly payment on what you actually earn, not just what you owe. On a $35,000 salary, a standard repayment plan might cost around $300 a month, while an income-driven plan on that same loan might cost closer to $90. Same debt, very different monthly payment. If money is tight in your first few years out of school, this option can help you stay current while you get established.

With graduated repayment, your payments start lower and they increase over time. It can work if you are confident your income will grow, but you will pay more in total interest than you would on the standard plan.

If you are going into public service work, there is one more option worth knowing about. If you work for a qualifying employer such as a government agency or nonprofit, you may be eligible for loan forgiveness after a set number of qualifying payments. The program is called Public Service Loan Forgiveness, and the rules are specific and have changed over the years. Read carefully and verify current requirements before you count on it.

What to Do Right Now

You do not need to have everything figured out today, but you do need to know your numbers. Start there.

Log in to studentaid.gov to find your federal loan information. Write down each loan's balance, interest rate, and servicer name. If you have private loans, check with your lender directly and add them to the same list. Then review your current repayment plan and research whether a different plan better fits your situation. Set up autopay if you have not already, since many servicers offer a small interest rate reduction for doing so. If you are already feeling behind, contact your servicer before you miss a payment. They have options, but they can only help if you reach out first.

Student loan debt is real and can feel heavy, but it is manageable with a plan. Ignoring it only makes it worse. Knowing your numbers, choosing the right repayment option, and making consistent payments protect your credit and keep you moving forward.

KEY INSIGHT: *The right repayment plan is not the most popular one or the one your friend chose. It is the one that fits your actual income and your actual life right now.*

SMALL STEP: *Do not try to solve your entire student loan situation this week. Just gather your exact balances.*

Riley (Common Sense) reminds you: "The right repayment plan is not the most common one or the one my friende I actually want to go."

TOOL 12: Career and Income Decisions

Most conversations about careers and money focus on one question: how do I earn more? That's a good question, but it's not the only one worth asking. The harder questions are worth thinking about: how do I earn enough without giving up the parts of my life that matter, and what do I actually want my days to look like?

This section isn't going to push you toward one path. Trades are great, and college is great, and both come with real trade-offs. The goal here is to help you think clearly about the financial picture before you commit to something that's hard to undo.

The Debt vs. Earning Potential Question

When you are deciding how much education or training to pursue, the most important financial question is what it will cost and what it will earn. A two-year associate's degree in nursing that costs $20,000 and leads to a $55,000 starting salary presents a very different financial picture than a four-year private university degree in a highly competitive field with a $38,000 starting salary and $80,000 in debt. Neither is automatically the wrong choice, but you should make it with your eyes open.

A useful rule of thumb: try not to borrow more in total student loans than you expect to earn in your first year of work. If you're going into teaching, try not to borrow more than a teacher's starting salary. If you're going into engineering, you have more room. This isn't a perfect formula, but it keeps the math from getting completely out of hand.

Trades vs. College: Both Are Real Paths

There's a persistent cultural idea that a four-year college degree is the right path and everything else is a backup plan, but that idea doesn't align with the job market or the financial reality. Skilled trades, including electricians, plumbers, HVAC technicians, welders, dental hygienists, and medical coders, are in high demand, often pay exceptionally well, and typically involve significantly less debt than a four-year degree. An electrician completing a five-year apprenticeship program often earns while learning, enters the field debt-free, and can reach $70,000 to $100,000 in income within a decade. That isn't a consolation prize but a real, well-compensated career with stable demand. The question isn't which path is better but which path fits your interests, your skills, and your financial situation.

Lifestyle Costs and Cost of Living

Where you live affects your finances as much as what you earn. A $50,000 salary in Duluth, a smaller town might leave you with more spending power and savings than a $70,000 salary in a large city like Minneapolis, and significantly more than that same salary in New York city, where rent alone can consume two-thirds of a paycheck. When you're comparing job offers or deciding where to settle, look at the actual cost of housing in that market. If rent requires more than 30% of your gross monthly income, you're going to feel squeezed no matter how excited you are about the job.

It's also worth considering longer-term questions, such as whether you want to own a home someday and what that market looks like in the city you're considering. These are forward-looking questions, but asking them now helps you avoid surprises later.

Side Jobs and Gig Work: Real Benefits, Real Trade-offs

Gig work is short-term, flexible, on-demand work, such as driving for a rideshare company, delivering food, freelancing, or selling things online. It can absolutely help you build income, especially when you're starting out. Gig workers are typically classified as independent contractors rather than employees, which means they have no employer-provided health insurance, no paid time off, no unemployment benefits if the work dries up, and no employer match on retirement savings. It also means you'll owe self-employment taxes at the end of the year, usually 15.3% on top of regular income taxes. Most platforms don't withhold those taxes for you, so set aside around 25% to 30% of what you earn from gig work to cover them. Gig work can be a great, flexible supplement to your income, but going in knowing it's not the same as traditional employment will help you plan accordingly.

One More Thing Nobody Tells You: Starting Salaries Are Negotiable

Most young adults accept the first salary they're offered because they don't realize they're allowed to ask for more. You are, and a simple, respectful question like "Is there any flexibility on the starting salary?" costs you nothing and can be worth thousands of dollars a year. That gap compounds over time because future raises are often calculated as a percentage of what you're already making. You don't have to be aggressive; you just have to ask.

Burnout and the Income vs. Freedom Trade-off

More money isn't always better. While that sounds obvious, it's easy to forget when you're 23 and trying to pay off debt and build savings as fast as possible. Some jobs pay more because they ask more of you, including longer hours, more stress, more of your identity, and more of your evenings and weekends. That trade-off can be worth it for a time, especially early in your career when you're building skills and financial stability, but it's important to be honest with yourself about how long you can sustain it. A job that pays $10,000 more per year than another option is the better financial choice if only the extra money doesn't cost you your health, your relationships, or your quality of life, because those things have real value even though they don't show up in a salary comparison.

Income Isn't Everything

Noor studied to become a social worker and knew going in that the starting salary was modest, around $38,000 a year. She also knew she'd kept her student debt to $22,000 by attending a state school and working summers. Five years out of school, she's not rich, but she has a paid-off car, no credit card debt, a small emergency fund, a 403(b) retirement account she contributes to steadily, and a job she finds genuinely meaningful. Compare that to a classmate who took a higher-paying corporate job at $58,000, assumed a much larger student loan burden to attend a more expensive school, moved to a high-cost city, and is now making more money but feeling financially stretched, overworked, and unsure whether the job is worth it. There's no moral to this story, and neither person is right or wrong. The point is that income level alone doesn't determine financial health, and the full picture, including debt load, cost of living, personal fulfillment, and sustainability, matters too.

KEY INSIGHT: *The highest-paying option is not always the best long-term choice. What you earn matters, and so does the cost of earning it.*

SMALL STEP: *Look up the average salary for three career paths you're considering, then find the average cost of a one-bedroom apartment in a city where those jobs are common, and ask yourself whether the math feels sustainable.*

Maya (Courage) reminds you: "Choosing a path that fits my life takes more courage than chasing the highest number. I get to decide what success looks like."

TOOL 13: Consumer Protection and Digital Money

You do more with your phone through your bank than any previous generation did. You send money to friends, pay for food, buy concert tickets, and manage your entire financial life through apps, and that's genuinely useful. It's also an environment full of traps that are easy to fall into. This section is about protecting yourself in that environment, not by avoiding it, but by knowing what to watch for.

Payment Apps: The Invisible Risk

Venmo, Cash App, Zelle, and similar services have one thing in common: they move money fast, and mistakes are hard to reverse. When you hand someone cash, you'd double-check the person before handing it over, and payment apps deserve the same attention.

Common mistakes people make with payment apps:

- **Sending to the wrong account.** Usernames are similar, and one typo means your $80 is gone. Always verify before you hit send, especially for larger amounts.
- **Falling for scammers posing as friends or sellers.** Someone claims to be selling event tickets or concert passes through a payment app. You send the money, and the tickets never arrive. Once you've sent the money, most apps won't reverse the transfer.
- **Leaving money in the app.** Your Venmo or Cash App balance is not FDIC-insured the way your bank account is, so keep your real savings in an actual bank account.

- **Accepting money from strangers.** If someone sends you money unexpectedly and asks you to send some back, that's almost always a scam. You can read more about how that works in Tool 5.

Subscription Traps

App stores and online services have become very good at making subscriptions easy to start and annoying to cancel. Common patterns to watch for include free trials that automatically convert to paid plans, annual subscriptions that renew silently on a date you've forgotten, pause options that feel like canceling but aren't, and services that require a phone call to cancel even though you signed up online. Once every three months, review your bank statement and look at every recurring charge. If you don't recognize it or can't remember the last time you used the service, cancel it. That fifteen minutes will save you money every month going forward.

Buy Now, Pay Later: Understand Before You Click

Buy Now, Pay Later services like Afterpay, Klarna, and Affirm let you split a purchase into smaller installments, often with no interest if you pay on time. They're genuinely useful in some situations, but there are a few things to know before you use them.

They're easy to stack, meaning you can have three or four active Buy Now, Pay Later plans running at the same time without feeling like you have any debt, because each individual payment is small. But add them up, and they can be a significant monthly obligation. Missing payments can mean late fees and, in some cases, hits to your credit score, because some Buy Now, Pay Later services now report to the credit bureaus, which means a missed payment can follow you. The no-interest offer is only no interest if you hit every payment on time. They also make it easier to buy things you'd otherwise pause on, which is by design. So if you were going to buy something anyway and the payments are truly interest-free, it's a neutral tool. But if the payment plan is what made the purchase feel possible, ask yourself whether you'd still want the item if you had to pay for it all at once today.

Online Fraud: The Most Common Forms

There's a tool dedicated to scams earlier in this book, but the short version is this: whenever something creates urgency and pushes you to act fast, that's exactly the moment to slow down and verify before you click, send, or share anything.

Account takeover is one of the most damaging forms of online fraud. It happens when someone gains access to your email or phone number and uses it to reset passwords on your financial accounts. Your email address and phone number are essentially the keys to your financial life, and protecting them is just as important as protecting your bank password.

For marketplace transactions, the general rule is that for significant amounts, cash or verified payment methods are safer than payment apps or personal checks. Sellers can disappear after you send a payment app transfer, and buyers can send checks for more than the agreed price and ask you to send the difference back.

Social Media and Financial Misinformation

Social media is full of financial advice. Some of it is genuinely useful, but much of it is wrong, oversimplified, or promoted by someone who benefits financially from you following it. Red flags for financial content on social media include promises of guaranteed returns or risk-free investments, urgency to act now before the opportunity disappears, advice designed to make you feel like an insider, people showing off expensive purchases and lifestyles as proof that their strategy works, and promotions for specific stocks, cryptocurrencies, or investment products without any disclosure of a financial relationship. This doesn't mean all financial content online is worthless, but apply the same skepticism you'd use with any stranger giving you advice about something important. Look for sources that are transparent about their credentials, don't have a financial stake in your decision, and explain their reasoning rather than just telling you what to do.

Protecting Your Accounts and Passwords

Your digital security is your financial security, and a few habits make a real difference. Use different passwords for different accounts. If you use the same password everywhere and one site gets hacked, everything gets hacked. Use a password manager. Trying to remember 20 different passwords is exactly why people use the same one everywhere, and a password manager stores them securely so you only have to remember one. Turn on two-factor authentication for your email, your bank, and your primary payment apps. It adds a second layer that makes it much harder for someone to get into your accounts, even if they have your password. Be careful on public Wi-Fi. Open networks at coffee shops, airports, and libraries are not secure, so avoid logging into financial accounts on public networks. Never share account credentials with anyone, including friends and family. If someone needs to access something, find another way.

Your Credit Card Protections

Credit cards can cause problems when used carelessly, but they also offer protections many young adults don't realize they have. If a charge appears that you didn't make, contact the credit card company immediately, lock or freeze the card if needed, review your recent transactions carefully, and document what happened. In many cases, consumers are protected against unauthorized charges if they report them promptly, which is one reason many financial experts recommend using a credit card for online purchases rather than a debit card. With a debit card, stolen money often leaves your bank account immediately, but with a credit card, the dispute process is generally easier and safer. That doesn't mean spend freely; it means understand how the system works and use it to your advantage.

Debt Collectors Have Rules Too

The consumer protections in this tool don't stop at your phone screen, they extend to anyone who contacts you about money you owe, and it's worth knowing your rights there too. If someone ever contacts you about a debt, stay calm, take notes, ask questions, and request information in writing. Some collectors are professional and respectful, but others may use pressure, fear, or intimidation. There are laws designed to protect consumers from abusive collection practices. Debt collectors generally cannot illegally threaten you, harass you repeatedly, pretend to be law enforcement, contact you at all hours, or lie about what you owe. If something feels wrong, pause and get help from a trusted adult, a financial professional, or a consumer protection agency. Never assume that a loud voice means someone is right.

Emotional Spending Online

Online shopping is engineered to make spending feel effortless and buying feel rewarding, with saved payment methods, one-click purchasing, and targeted ads that show you exactly what you were just thinking about. All of it is designed to reduce the friction between you and a purchase. There's nothing wrong with buying things online, but it's worth knowing that the ease of the experience is by design and that the emotional state you're in when you shop affects what you buy. Late-night browsing, scrolling when you're stressed or bored, and shopping after a bad day are the moments when it's easiest to add things to a cart that you wouldn't have bought in a calmer moment. The 48-hour rule from earlier in this book is especially useful in these situations: leave the item in the cart, check back in two days, and if you still want it and you have the money, buy it. If you forgot you added it, that tells you something.

KEY INSIGHT: *The digital world is built for speed, but your financial health benefits from slowing down. One pause before you tap, one look at the full subscription list, and one moment to verify before you send. These small habits protect you in ways that take almost no time.*

SMALL STEP: *This week, review your bank or credit card statement and find every recurring charge. List them and cancel any subscription you haven't used in the last 30 days.*

Jordan (Balance) reminds you: "The digital world is designed for speed. I protect myself by slowing down just long enough to think."

TOOL 14: Taxes—What You Need to Know Before You File

Taxes can feel overwhelming until someone explains them. Once you understand the basic system, they're just paperwork with rules that make sense. This section won't make you a tax expert, but it will make sure you're not blindsided the first time you have to file on your own.

The Basic Idea

When you earn money, the government takes a portion of it to fund public services, including roads, schools, emergency services, and more. How much you owe depends on how much you earn and where the money came from. Most people pay taxes in two ways: a little at a time throughout the year, withheld automatically from each paycheck, and then a final accounting in the spring called filing your tax return. Filing is how you and the government settle up. If too much was withheld, you get a refund, but if not enough was withheld, you owe the difference.

The Two Documents You Need to Know

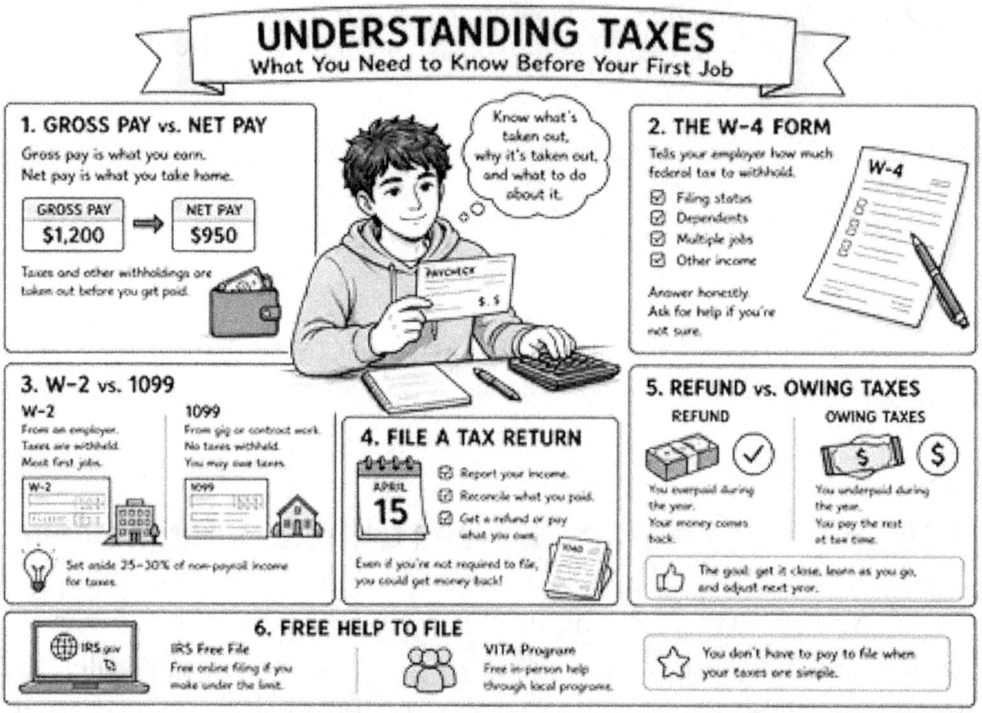

- **W-2:** If you work for an employer, the employer is required to send you a W-2 form by the end of January each year. It shows exactly how much you earned and how much was withheld for taxes, and it is the main document you need to file your return.
- **1099:** If you did gig work, freelance jobs, or any work where you were paid as an independent contractor rather than an employee, you will likely receive a 1099 form instead. The key difference is that no taxes were withheld from that money, meaning you earned it in full and now you owe taxes on it. Many first-time gig workers are caught off guard by this. If you earned more than $600 from a single source as an independent contractor, that source is required to send you a 1099. If you earned less than that from one source, you may not receive a form, even though you still owe taxes on the income. A simple rule: if someone paid you to do work this year, assume it counts as taxable income until you learn otherwise.

When and How to File

The federal tax deadline is April 15 most years, and your state may have its own deadline, though it usually matches the federal one. Failing to file for an extension by the deadline can result in penalties, so mark it on your calendar early.

If your taxes are straightforward, meaning you have a W-2 from one employer, no investments, and no major life changes, you can likely file for free. The IRS Free File program at irs.gov offers free filing for people who qualify based on income, and many young adults qualify without even knowing it. If you have a 1099, multiple jobs, or a more complicated situation, tax software like TurboTax, H&R Block, or FreeTaxUSA can walk you through the process step by step at low or no cost, depending on your situation. If your taxes feel genuinely complicated, a tax preparer or accountant is worth the cost for at least the first year, because watching someone walk through your return once teaches you more than reading about it ever will.

One thing worth knowing: filing your taxes and paying your taxes are two separate things. Even if you cannot afford to pay what you owe right now, file anyway. The penalty for not filing is steeper than the penalty for filing and paying late.

If You Did Gig Work or Freelance Work

This is the part that surprises most people the first time. When you work for an employer, the employer pays half of your Social Security and Medicare taxes, but when you work for yourself, even part time, you pay both halves. This is called self-employment tax, which runs about 15.3% on top of your regular income tax. Knowing that number ahead of time is what keeps it from becoming a crisis. The simplest way to handle it is to set aside 25% to 30% of every independent work payment in a separate account and not touch it. When tax time comes, that money is already waiting. Most people who get into trouble with self-employment taxes have spent the money before the bill arrived and had no way to cover it.

If you earn significant income from self-employment, you may also be required to make quarterly estimated tax payments throughout the year rather than settling up all at once in April, and the IRS website has a tool to help you figure out whether this applies to you.

KEY INSIGHT: *Taxes are not complicated because they are hard; they are complicated because nobody explains them. Once you understand the basic system, filing on your own is manageable. Knowing what you owe before the bill arrives keeps taxes from becoming a crisis.*

SMALL STEP: *Find last year's tax return if you have one, or look up your W-2 or 1099 from your most recent job. Find the line that shows what you earned and what was withheld, because understanding those two numbers is where everything else starts.*

Owen (Clarity) reminds you: "Taxes feel mysterious until you look at the actual numbers. Once I understand what I owe and why, I can plan for it. Confusion is the only thing that makes this hard."

TOOL 15: Investing Basics

Saving money and investing money are not the same thing. Saving helps protect money you may need soon, while investing helps money grow over long periods of time. Both matter. Many young adults hear people talk about investing, but nobody really explains it clearly, and the language can sound confusing or intimidating when you first encounter it. It doesn't need to be, and you don't need to become a stock market expert to be a successful long-term investor. You simply need to understand a few important ideas and make thoughtful decisions consistently over time.

Your Greatest Advantage Is Time

One of the greatest advantages you have as a young adult is not your income, and it's not perfect knowledge about the market. It's time. When people begin investing early, even small amounts can grow significantly over the years because of something called compound growth, which is what happens when the money you've invested begins earning money of its own, and then those earnings begin earning money too. That process takes years to build real momentum, which is exactly why starting early matters so much more than starting with a large amount. Many people believe investing is only for wealthy adults later in life, but small, steady investing habits started early often outperform large amounts invested much later.

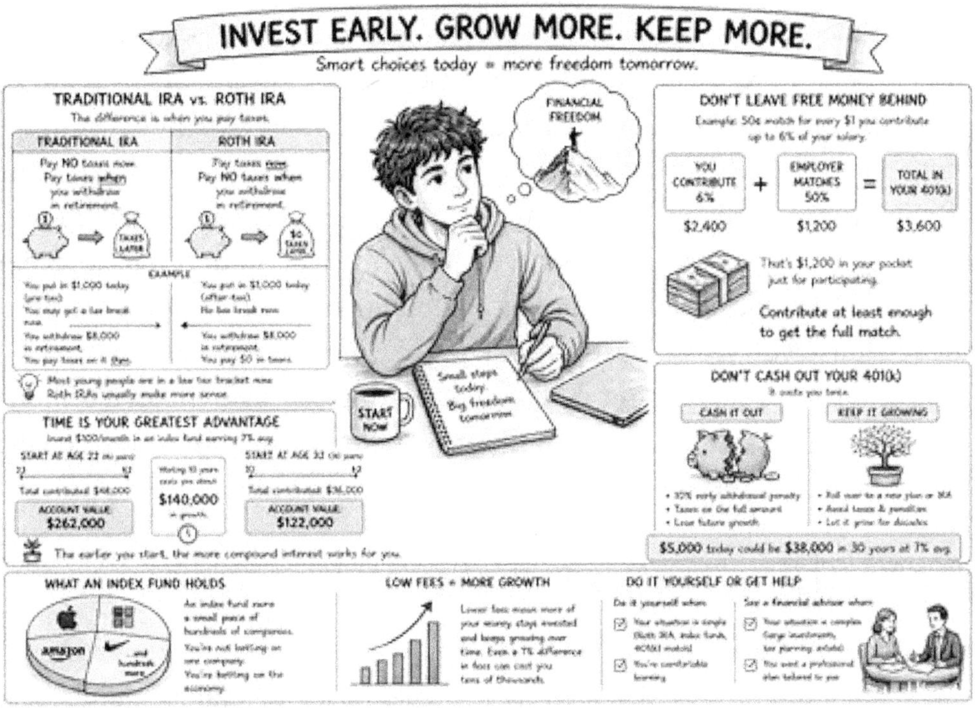

Don't Put Everything in One Basket

You've probably heard the advice "don't put all your eggs in one basket," and that applies directly to investing. Different investments rise and fall in value at different times. Some years one area of the market performs well while other years it struggles. Spreading your investments across different types of assets rather than depending on just one thing is called diversification, and it's one of the most important habits a long-term investor can build. Imagine two people: one invests everything in a single company after hearing excitement about it online, and another spreads investments across many companies and industries through broader funds. The second approach is generally safer and more stable over long periods of time. While diversification doesn't guarantee success, it helps reduce the risk that one bad decision could cause major damage to everything you've built.

Understanding Asset Allocation

Asset allocation is the mix of investments you choose to hold. The most common categories are stocks, bonds, and cash or savings. Stocks generally offer greater long-term growth potential, but they also fluctuate more noticeably from year to year. Bonds are usually steadier but often grow more slowly. Cash is stable and useful for short-term needs, but it typically grows the least over time. Young adults often hear the advice to take more risk when you're young, and there's some truth to that because younger investors have more time to recover from market declines. But every person is different, and good investing isn't about chasing excitement. It's about building a plan that matches your goals, your timeline, and your comfort level with uncertainty.

Fees Matter More Than Most People Realize

One of the most overlooked parts of investing is fees. Many investments carry small ongoing costs, such as expense ratios or management fees, that quietly erode your long-term growth in ways that are hard to see until you do the math. One percent here and half a percent there might not sound like a big deal, but over many years those fees can shave thousands, even tens of thousands, off your long-term results. Think of it as carrying a slightly heavier backpack on a very long hike.

Even a little extra weight adds up over time. This doesn't mean every paid financial service is bad. Some people benefit greatly from trusted financial guidance, but always ask what the fees are, how the person advising you gets paid, and whether you genuinely understand what you're buying.

Tax-Advantaged Accounts Are Worth Understanding

Some investment accounts offer special tax advantages designed to encourage long-term saving. You don't need to memorize every rule, but understanding the basics can save you a significant amount of money over time. A Roth IRA lets you invest money that has already been taxed, and if you follow the rules, the growth and withdrawals later in life may be completely tax-free, a real advantage for anyone who starts early. Many workplaces also offer retirement accounts such as a 401(k), and some employers even provide a matching contribution, meaning they add money to your account simply because you participate. Not taking full advantage of an employer match is often described as turning down part of your compensation, because that's essentially what it is.

Markets Go Up and Down, and That's Normal

The growth of investments is not a straight line. Markets rise and fall, sometimes quickly and sometimes dramatically, which can feel uncomfortable when it's happening to money you've worked hard to save. Many people make poor investing decisions because of emotion, panicking during declines, getting overexcited during booms, fearing they're missing out, or trying to predict every market movement. All of those reactions tend to cost money over time. Long-term investing generally rewards patience far more than constant reacting does, and the most successful investors are often not the smartest people in the room but simply those who stayed steady when everyone else was panicking.

Before You Invest, Ask These Questions

Before putting money into any investment, it's worth slowing down to make sure you can honestly answer a few basic questions: Do you understand what this is and how it makes money? What are the risks and costs? Are you investing based on a plan or reacting to something you saw online? A calm, informed decision is almost always stronger than an emotional one. If you can't explain what you're investing in and why, that's a signal to keep learning before you commit. That applies to everything, including cryptocurrency, which some people choose to invest in, it's more volatile than most traditional investments, so it deserves every one of those same questions, maybe more.

KEY INSIGHT: *The most powerful investing advantage young adults have is time. Starting early with small, consistent contributions almost always outperforms waiting until you have more money. You don't need to be wealthy to start, and you don't need to be an expert. You just need to begin.*

SMALL STEP: *Check whether your employer offers a 401(k) match and whether you're taking full advantage of it. If you don't have an employer plan yet, spend fifteen minutes this week reading about what a Roth IRA is and what it takes to open one. You don't have to do it today, but understanding the option is the first step toward using it.*

Lin (Time Perspective) reminds you: "The best time to start investing was yesterday, and the second best time is today. I don't need a lot of money to begin, I just need to begin, because time is the one advantage I have right now that I can never get back."

TOOL 16: How to Make Better Financial Decisions

Most financial problems aren't caused by a lack of intelligence but by rushed decisions, emotional reactions, pressure, and simply not slowing down long enough to think clearly before acting. That's encouraging news, because it means the skill that matters most here isn't how smart you are but how aware you are. Awareness is something anyone can build with practice.

One of this book's main goals has been to help you think more clearly about money, because every financial decision moves your life in some direction, and even small ones add up over time.

Every Decision Has Trade-Offs

In life, choosing one thing often means giving up something else, and that's called a tradeoff. Understanding trade-offs is one of the most useful financial habits you can develop. When you spend money on one thing, that money can't also go somewhere else. This doesn't mean spending is bad; it simply means that choices have consequences worth thinking about before you make them. Going out to eat may leave less money for travel later; buying a more expensive car may affect future housing choices; working extra hours may provide more income but less personal time; and saving money now may create more freedom later. Life is full of trade-offs, and wise decision makers learn to notice them clearly rather than discovering them after the fact.

Understanding Opportunity Cost

Opportunity cost is one of the most important financial concepts you can learn. It means that when you choose one option, you also give up the opportunity to use that same time, money, or energy for something else. Sometimes the cost is obvious, and sometimes it's hidden, but it's always there. Imagine spending $120 every month on subscriptions, food delivery, or impulse purchases that don't add much to your life. That may not seem significant in the moment, but over time that same money could have become an emergency fund, a car repair cushion, travel opportunities, investment contributions, or simply less financial stress and more freedom. This doesn't mean you should never spend money on enjoyable things. It simply means asking yourself what you're giving up in exchange for each choice, because that question alone can improve many financial decisions.

Cost-Benefit Thinking

Opportunity cost and cost-benefit thinking are cousins. Both help you see the full picture of a decision, but where opportunity cost asks what you're giving up, cost-benefit thinking asks whether the whole trade is worth it.

Cost-benefit thinking, which means looking at the positives, the negatives, the risks, and the possible long-term effects of a decision before you make it. A cheaper apartment may save money each month, but if it creates a stressful commute, safety concerns, or constant transportation problems, the cheapest option may not be the best overall choice when you add everything up. Or imagine buying something expensive on impulse, where the short-term benefit is excitement but the long-term cost may be debt, stress, or delayed goals that mattered more than the purchase. Good decision makers try to look at the full picture rather than just the immediate feeling. Building that habit early saves a lot of regret later.

Short-Term Feelings vs. Long-Term Goals

One of the hardest parts of managing money well is balancing what you want now with what you're working toward over time. There's nothing wrong with wanting comfort, fun, convenience, and enjoyment in the present, and the challenge is making sure those short-term emotions don't consistently overpower the longer-term priorities that matter most to you. Many strong financial decisions involve delayed gratification, which means choosing to wait today to create something better later. Examples show up everywhere: saving before buying, building an emergency fund, investing consistently, and avoiding unnecessary debt all require some patience in the present in exchange for more freedom in the future. Future You is affected by the decisions Current You makes every day, and that's why awareness matters so much.

Emotional Spending Is Real

People don't always spend money logically, and it's worth understanding that about yourself rather than being surprised by it. Sometimes people spend because they're stressed, lonely, bored, tired, frustrated, trying to impress others, or simply trying to feel better temporarily. There's nothing shameful about that, because it's a very human response to difficult moments. Advertisements and social media are specifically designed to encourage emotional spending. While treating yourself occasionally is harmless, the habit, when repeated constantly, can quietly damage financial progress in ways that are hard to see until you look at a month of transactions and add them up. One of the healthiest financial habits you can build is learning to pause before you make emotional purchases, because even a short delay creates enough space to think clearly about whether you actually want something or just feel like buying it right now.

A Simple Way to Think Before You Decide

When a financial decision is in front of you, slow the process down before you act. The framework is simple: Study the situation by asking what you actually know and what information you might be missing. Think it through by considering the trade-offs, the risks, the opportunity cost, and how this choice might affect Future You. Then decide. After working through those questions honestly, trust yourself to make the wisest choice you can with what you know right now. That process sounds simple because it is simple, and many good decisions are built on exactly that kind of straightforward thinking, applied consistently over time.

You Don't Have to Be Perfect

Everyone makes financial mistakes, including people who are genuinely good with money. The goal is not to be perfec but to improve your awareness and decision-making a little at a time. A thoughtful person who learns from mistakes will almost always make better long-term decisions than someone who constantly reacts emotionally without pausing to reflect. Your financial future is shaped less by one giant decision and more by hundreds of small decisions repeated over time. The good news is that you don't need to control everything perfectly. You simply want to become someone who pauses before reacting, considers consequences, recognizes trade-offs, learns from mistakes, and keeps moving forward with a little more clarity each time.

KEY INSIGHT: *Most financial mistakes aren't caused by a lack of intelligence; they're caused by not slowing down long enough to think clearly. The habit of pausing before you decide, even for a moment, is one of the most valuable financial skills you can build, and it gets easier with each use.*

SMALL STEP: *Think about one financial decision you're currently facing, something real, whether it's a purchase you're considering, a subscription you haven't canceled, or a savings goal you haven't started. Run it through the Study, Think, Decide framework in this tool. You don't have to act on anything today, but thinking it through clearly is exactly the kind of practice that builds better financial habits over time.*

Aalaya (Goals) reminds you: "Every financial decision I make is either moving me toward what I actually want or pulling me away from it. When I slow down long enough to remember my goals, the right choice usually becomes a lot clearer."

PART 5

My Start Smart Financial Plan

Pulling It All Together

You've covered a lot of ground in this course. You've honestly examined the money messages you grew up with. You've built a budget, opened or considered opening a bank account, learned how credit works, and begun to distinguish between what you want and what you actually need. That's not a small thing. Most adults never do this work in any organized way.

This section asks you to pull it all together, not to impress anyone with a perfect financial plan, but to leave this course with something real: a written picture of where you are, where you want to go, and a few specific steps you can take. You'll work through five sections, each building on the last. By the time you reach the end, you'll have something worth keeping.

CAM Retake: Your Check-In

You took this assessment at the start of the course. Now take it again before you look at your previous scores, and answer based on what's true for you right now. When you're done, refer back to your Chapter 5 CAM Check-In and compare your results.

How to Rate Yourself: *Circle one number for each statement:*

1 = Not true at all | **2** = A little true | **3** = Sometimes true
4 = Mostly true | **5** = Very true

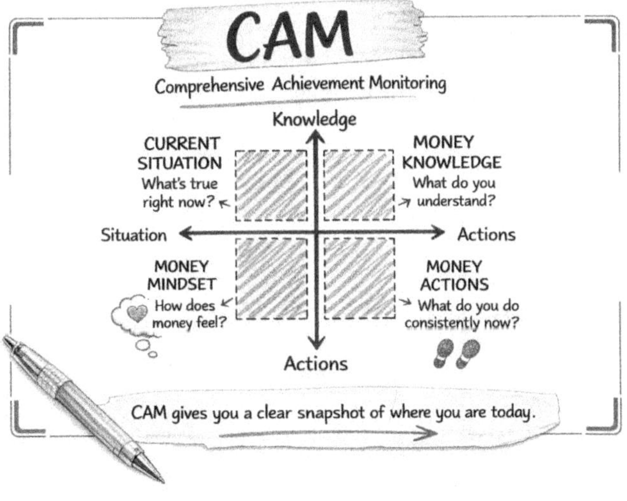

Part 1: Your Current Situation

1. I have a sense of how much money comes in from things like allowance, gifts, or a job.	1 · 2 · 3 · 4 · 5
2. I have a sense of where my money goes, such as food, clothes, subscriptions, or going out.	1 · 2 · 3 · 4 · 5
3. I have a bank account I use, such as a checking or savings account.	1 · 2 · 3 · 4 · 5
4. I check my balance regularly, whether through an app, online, or at the bank.	1 · 2 · 3 · 4 · 5
5. I have a sense of whether I'm spending more or less than I have.	1 · 2 · 3 · 4 · 5
6. I understand what I actually take home from a paycheck after taxes and deductions.	1 · 2 · 3 · 4 · 5
7. I know if I owe money, such as a credit card balance, student loan, or money borrowed.	1 · 2 · 3 · 4 · 5
8. I feel some level of clarity about my money right now, even if it's still developing.	1 · 2 · 3 · 4 · 5
9. I know who I owe and when payments are due, such as credit cards, loans, or other bills.	1 · 2 · 3 · 4 · 5
10. I have a basic understanding of what a credit score is and why it matters.	1 · 2 · 3 · 4 · 5
Section Score (add your numbers 10–50)	**______ / 50**

Part 2: Your Money Knowledge

1. I understand the difference between a checking account and a savings account.	1 · 2 · 3 · 4 · 5
2. I understand how interest works when saving money or borrowing money.	1 · 2 · 3 · 4 · 5
3. I understand what a credit score is and how it can affect things like loans or renting.	1 · 2 · 3 · 4 · 5
4. I understand how student loans work and what I need to pay attention to.	1 · 2 · 3 · 4 · 5
5. I understand what a simple plan for spending money looks like.	1 · 2 · 3 · 4 · 5
6. I understand how money can grow over time through saving or investing.	1 · 2 · 3 · 4 · 5
7. I understand the difference between using a debit card and a credit card.	1 · 2 · 3 · 4 · 5
8. I know what renters insurance is and what it covers	1 · 2 · 3 · 4 · 5
9. I understand that there are ways to save and invest for the future, such as a 401(k) or IRA.	1 · 2 · 3 · 4 · 5
10. I understand how to read a basic pay stub and what the different parts mean.	1 · 2 · 3 · 4 · 5

Section Score (add your numbers 10–50) ______ **/ 50**

Part 3: Your Money Mindset

1. I believe I can improve my money situation over time.	1 · 2 · 3 · 4 · 5
2. When I think about money, I feel more curious than stressed.	1 · 2 · 3 · 4 · 5
3. I am willing to look at my account or money situation, even if it feels uncomfortable.	1 · 2 · 3 · 4 · 5
4. I believe past mistakes with money do not define my future.	1 · 2 · 3 · 4 · 5
5. I feel capable of learning what I don't yet know about money.	1 · 2 · 3 · 4 · 5
6. I am aware of how often I compare myself to others when it comes to money.	1 · 2 · 3 · 4 · 5
7. I believe small steps can make a real difference over time.	1 · 2 · 3 · 4 · 5
8. I feel some sense of hope about my financial future.	1 · 2 · 3 · 4 · 5
9. I tend to think things through before spending money.	1 · 2 · 3 · 4 · 5
10. I believe I deserve to feel stable and at peace with my money.	1 · 2 · 3 · 4 · 5
Section Score (add your numbers 10–50)	**______ / 50**

Part 4: Your Money Actions

1. I have some money set aside for unexpected expenses, like a car repair. 1 · 2 · 3 · 4 · 5
2. I pay bills on time when I have them, such as a phone bill, subscription fee, or credit card bill. 1 · 2 · 3 · 4 · 5
3. I keep track of my spending in some way, such as using an app, keeping notes, or checking my account. 1 · 2 · 3 · 4 · 5
4. I have some savings, even if it's a small amount set aside over time. 1 · 2 · 3 · 4 · 5
5. I think carefully before taking on debt for things I don't truly need. 1 · 2 · 3 · 4 · 5
6. I look at my account activity regularly, such as reviewing transactions or balances. 1 · 2 · 3 · 4 · 5
7. I have something I'm saving for, like a car, school expenses, travel, or something important to me. 1 · 2 · 3 · 4 · 5
8. I make intentional choices about what I spend money on, such as needs versus wants. 1 · 2 · 3 · 4 · 5
9. I ask questions or look for reliable information when I'm unsure about money. 1 · 2 · 3 · 4 · 5
10. I am taking steps to improve my money situation right now, even if they are small. 1 · 2 · 3 · 4 · 5

Section Score (add your numbers 10–50) ______ **/ 50**

Your Total CAM Snapshot
Add your four section scores together (40–200): ____________

- **40–80** → Just Starting
- **81–120** → Building Awareness
- **121–160** → Developing Confidence
- **161–200** → Making a Strong Foundation

What surprised me:

____

____

One area where I'm stronger than I thought:

____

____

One area where I want to grow:

____

____

One small step I can take this week:

____

____

SECTION 1

Where I Am Now

Revisiting Your CAM Check-In

Refer back to your Chapter 5 CAM Check-In. Review the numbers you gave yourself at the start of this course and compare them with the scores you just recorded. Then write a short, honest reflection of two to four paragraphs that answers these questions:

What has changed for you since you filled that out? Have any of your scores changed? Which areas feel more solid now?

____

____

What surprised you as you moved through the material? Was there a tool or principle that stood out more than you expected?

____

____

Where do you still feel unsure or underprepared? Be specific. Saying "I'm not great at saving" doesn't count. What specifically is hard about it for you?

____

____

____

____

Write your reflection in the space below, or on a separate sheet your teacher provides.

SECTION 2

My Money Story

Summarizing What You Learned About Yourself

Early in this course, you explored money messages, the messages you heard and absorbed about money growing up. You also examined limiting beliefs, the thoughts that quietly shape your financial behavior, even when you're not aware of them.

In this section, write two to three paragraphs that cover:

- At least one money message from your upbringing, including where it came from and whether you still believe it
- At least one limiting belief you identified about yourself and money, and the reframe you practiced
- Whether that reframe has changed how you think or act, even slightly

This doesn't need to be dramatic or deeply personal; it just needs to be honest. You're not being graded on what you believe, but on whether you actually looked.

SECTION 3

My Financial Picture

Net Worth Snapshot and Monthly Budget

This section has two parts. Use your actual numbers if you have them. If you're not yet working, use $2,500 as your estimated monthly take-home pay. That's a reasonable starting point for a full-time entry-level position.

Part A: Net Worth Snapshot

List your assets (what you own) and your liabilities (what you owe). Subtract liabilities from assets. The result, whether positive or negative, is your current net worth. There's no wrong answer. Starting at zero or below is completely normal at your age. The point is to know your number and understand what it means.

Examples of assets: *savings account balance, checking account balance, a car you own, anything else of value you own outright*

Examples of liabilities: *any debt you currently owe, a loan on a car, credit card balances, anything you'll need to pay back*

ASSETS (what you own)

Savings account balance: $____
Checking account balance: $____
Car or other property: $____
Other: $____

Total Assets: $______________

LIABILITIES (what you owe)

Credit card balance: $____
Car loan or other loan: $____
Money borrowed from others: $____
Other: $____

Total Liabilities: $________________

Net Worth (Assets minus Liabilities): $ ________________

Part B: Monthly Budget Using 50/30/20

Use the framework from Tool 8. If you're using $2,500 as your income, here's how the split looks:

- Needs (50%) = $1,250
- Wants (30%) = $750
- Savings and Debt Payoff (20%) = $500

Use your own income if you have it. In any case, note what goes in each category.

Monthly take-home income: $________________

Needs (50% = $_______________**):** What's included?

Wants (30% = $_______________**):** What's included?

Savings & Debt Payoff (20% = $______________**):** What's included?

SECTION 4

My Goals and My Plan

Where I'm Headed and What I'll Do Next

Write one financial goal for each of these time horizons: one year from now, three years from now, and five years from now. Each goal should be specific and grounded. "I want to have more money" doesn't count. "I want to have $500 in an emergency fund by June of next year" counts. If you're already working full-time, set your target at $1,500. The goal is the same either way: start building a cushion before you need one.

My one-year goal:

____

____

____

My three-year goal:

____

____

____

My five-year goal:

____

____

____

____

For your one-year goal, write at least three specific actions you'll take in the next 30 days, not someday, not eventually, but the next 30 days. Write them as concrete commitments:

I will:

____

____

____

____

I will:

____

____

____

____

I will:

____

____

____

____

If your three- or five-year goals align with topics from this course, such as building credit, investing, or buying a car, note which tools or principles support those goals.

____

____

____

____

SECTION 5

One Thing I'll Teach

Connecting to Principle 9

Principle 9 is Teach It Forward. The premise is simple: **you don't truly own knowledge until you've shared it. When you share what you've learned with someone who needs it, you both benefit.**

1. Identify one person in your life who could genuinely benefit from something you learned in this course. It might be a younger sibling, a parent, a friend, or a cousin. You know who it is.

Who I chose:

____

2. Write what you would say to them as if you were sitting across from them. Not a summary of the book. A real conversation. What would you start with? What example would make it click for them?

____

____

____

____

____

____

____

____

____

3. Write two or three sentences explaining why you chose that person. What about their situation or your relationship makes you the right person to share this? *This section doesn't need to be long. It needs to be real.*

____

____

____

____

____

____

Before You Close This Book

You did the work. Most people spend their entire lives reacting to money, stressed, behind on it, and confused by it, because no one ever gave them a structured chance to think it through. You had that chance, and you took it seriously. What you've built here isn't a finished plan. It's a starting point, and starting points are exactly what they sound like. The next step is yours. Take it.

For my children and grandchildren—
you are why this matters.

A Note from Kay

If you're reading this right now, here's what I want you to know: finishing a book like this already says something important about you. Most people avoid money conversations for as long as they can, putting them off and hoping things somehow work themselves out, or convincing themselves they'll deal with it later. You chose to stop and pay attention to something that will affect nearly every part of your life moving forward.

Over the years, I watched many students walk into my classroom convinced they weren't capable—some believed they weren't musical enough, some thought they were already behind, and many quietly assumed that everyone else understood things more quickly than they did. Most of the time, what they needed wasn't talent or perfection but perspective, practice, patience, and someone willing to help them see things a little more clearly.

Money works that way too.

I've watched people completely change the direction of their financial lives, not because something dramatic happened overnight but because they finally understood one important thing and decided to act on it. Sometimes that meant opening a savings account for the first time, sometimes it meant paying attention to where their money was actually going instead of avoiding it, and sometimes it simply meant asking a question they had been too embarrassed to ask before.

Small choices rarely feel powerful in the moment, yet over time they shape almost everything.

We've talked a lot about zooming in and zooming out to see the big picture, about balance, habits, and goals, about pressure and confidence, and about the quiet stories people carry about money and themselves. I don't want you to walk away thinking you need to have everything figured out—none of us do. I hope instead that you leave this book understanding that financial confidence grows from paying attention, thinking clearly, asking better questions, and continuing to move forward even when life still feels uncertain.

You've got the glasses now. Keep them on.

I believe in you,

Kay Hawley

Start Smart
Quick Start Checklist

You don't have to do everything at once. Find where you are right now, pick one item, do it this week, and come back for the next one.

When You Get Your First Job

- ❒ Set up direct deposit so your paycheck goes straight to your bank account.
- ❒ Find out your net take-home pay after taxes before you spend a single dollar.
- ❒ Look at your pay stub and identify every deduction so nothing surprises you.
- ❒ If anything on your pay stub is unclear, ask your HR department
- ❒ Find out if your employer offers a 401(k) and whether they match contributions.

When You Open Your First Bank Account

- ❒ Choose a checking account with no monthly fees and no minimum balance requirement.
- ❒ Open a separate savings account the same day and label it your emergency fund.
- ❒ Set up an automatic transfer to savings, even $5 or $10 a paycheck is a real start.
- ❒ Download your bank's app and check your balance once a week.
- ❒ Ask about overdraft protection and understand exactly how it works before you need it.
- ❒ Know your account number and routing number and where to find them.

If You Already Have a Job and a Bank Account

- ❒ List every recurring subscription and cancel anything you haven't used in 30 days.
- ❒ Track your spending for one full month so you know where your money actually goes.

- ❐ Create a simple monthly budget using the 50/30/20 framework from Tool 8.
- ❐ Set a first emergency fund goal of $200, then work toward $500.
- ❐ Increase your automatic savings transfer by $5 or more every time you get a raise or extra hours.

When You Get Your First Credit Card

- ❐ Pay the full balance every month if at all possible.
- ❐ Set up autopay for at least the minimum payment so you never miss a due date.
- ❐ Keep your balance below 30% of your credit limit.
- ❐ Do not apply for multiple cards at once.
- ❐ Remember: a credit card is a payment tool, not extra money.

When You Sign Your First Lease

- ❐ Read the entire lease before you sign, every page.
- ❐ Ask what utilities are included and which ones are your responsibility.
- ❐ Find out the early termination penalty before you need it.
- ❐ Document everything on move-in day with photos and send them to your landlord in writing.
- ❐ Get renter's insurance before you move in, it costs less than a streaming subscription.

When You Start Thinking About a Car

- ❐ Calculate the total monthly cost: payment, insurance, gas, and maintenance.
- ❐ Consider a reliable used car before assuming you need something new.
- ❐ Avoid financing longer than four years.
- ❐ Get pre-approved for a loan before you start shopping.
- ❐ If the payment makes you nervous, the car is too expensive.

When You Want to Protect Yourself

- ❐ Never give out your Social Security number, bank login, or PIN to anyone who contacts you first.

- ❒ Learn the warning signs of a scam: urgency, gift cards, threats, and offers that seem too good.
- ❒ Set up two-factor authentication on your email and all banking apps.
- ❒ Use different passwords for different accounts or use a password manager.
- ❒ If you think you've been scammed, call your bank immediately and don't wait.

When You're Ready to Check Your Credit

- ❒ Pull your free credit report at AnnualCreditReport.com.
- ❒ Review it for accounts you don't recognize or errors that look wrong.
- ❒ Dispute anything incorrect directly with the credit bureau.
- ❒ Understand the five factors that affect your score: payment history, utilization, length, mix, and new credit.
- ❒ Know that your score is not a grade on your worth. It reflects your habits, and habits can change.

When You're Ready to Think About the Future

- ❒ Look up what a Roth IRA is and what it takes to open one.
- ❒ Start small: even $10 a month invested consistently is better than waiting.
- ❒ Understand the difference between saving and investing and why both matter.
- ❒ Set one financial goal for the next six months and write it down somewhere you will see it.
- ❒ Run big decisions through the Study, Think, Decide framework from Tool 16.

One Last Thing

- ❒ Identify one person in your life you can teach something from this book.
- ❒ Share one tool, one principle, or one idea that changed how you think.

Acknowledgments

This book is better because people believed in it before it was finished.

Dave Braaten and his students at Hopkins High School gave this book something no editor could: honest, real-world feedback from the exact readers it was written for. Their energy and candor pushed me in ways I did not expect. I left that classroom with pages of notes and a much clearer sense of what this book needed to become. Those 67 students made the language more inclusive and the stories more authentic. They are the reason *The Quiet Student* moved from the back of the book to the front. They connected with it so strongly that it had to open the section rather than close it. I am deeply grateful to Dave and to every student who gave their time and their honesty.

To the early readers who gave their time, their feedback, and in some cases their own words to these pages, especially Terri Osland and Brett Smith. Your voices are in this book, and I am grateful for that.

To my production team, Connie Anderson of Words & Deeds, Inc., and Melissa Williams of Melissa Williams Design: thank you for bringing skill, patience, and professionalism to every page.

Beth Anderson of Plum-Creek.com built kayhawley.com and gave this work a home online. The site looks the way it does because of her patience and her eye for design.

Thanks also to Marcy Traxler, who helped me prepare the illustration files for print.

To the many friends, colleagues, and readers who encouraged this work along the way, including the West Women Investors, the Gurus, and the hundreds of teachers who sat in my Financial Awareness classes over the years: you were always the reason this needed to be written down. You know who you are, and so do I.

To those who trusted me with private consultations over the years: those hours shaped this book as much as anything else.

To my husband Dave, who never once suggested I stop, and who quietly made everything easier so I could keep going: thank you.

To my children, grandchildren, former students, and the many friends who have walked alongside me through this work: you are the reason any of it matters.

This book began with a simple belief: that every young adult deserves a fair start with money. I hope it delivers on that.

About the Author

Kay Hawley believes that a rich life begins with an understanding of how money really works.

An award-winning educator, Kay was recognized as Minnesota Music Educator of the Year and received the Northfield High School Distinguished Alumni Award. She spent more than thirty-five years in the classroom learning how young people build confidence, develop skills, and discover what they are truly capable of. She is known for her ability to take complex, intimidating ideas and make them clear, approachable, and genuinely useful.

Her passion for financial literacy is personal. Kay grew up in a large family with limited resources, so she knows firsthand what it feels like to worry about money and to wish someone had explained things sooner. Later in her career, while teaching financial awareness classes for fellow educators and community members, she discovered that many adults—hardworking, capable people—had never been taught how money actually works either.

That realization became Start Smart Money Basics: the book she wishes someone had handed to her when she was young. Independent of any investment firm, Kay combines a lifetime in education with real-world financial experience to help young adults build confidence with money and the freedom to shape lives of purpose and possibility.

Kay approaches financial literacy the same way she approached teaching music: start where you are, pay attention to the fundamentals, and improve steadily through small, consistent actions practiced over time. The CAM Check-In, the Ferris Wheel, and the microscope-and-telescope "special glasses" approach all grew out of her years in the classroom.

Today, Kay is living her second act on the water, competing in fishing tournaments, guiding, and leading fishing camps in the Canadian wilderness. She believes true richness isn't just about money, it's the freedom to build a life full of purpose and possibility.

She lives in Minnesota with her husband, Dave.

Connect With Kay

For Readers

I would love to hear from you.

If something in this book helped you think differently about money, or if you still have a question you are carrying, please reach out. You can learn more at kayhawley.com.

I read every message and answer as many as I can.

For Educator and Organizations

Kay Hawley is available for:

- School visits
- Financial literacy workshops
- Keynote presentations
- Educator training
- Private financial consultations

For speaking inquiries or to learn more about the Start Smart series, visit kayhawley.com.

Thank You

Thank you for reading *Start Smart Money Basics.*

My hope is that this book helps young adults feel more confident, prepared, and free as they begin making real-life money decisions.

If you found this book helpful, I would truly appreciate a brief review on Amazon. Your review helps other students, parents, teachers, and schools discover the book.

A review link and QR code will be available soon at: kayhawley.com

Thank you again for your support and encouragement.

—Kay Hawley

"This isn't about getting rich. It's about getting free."

About the Start Smart Series

Start Smart Money Basics — Book 1

10 Money Principles Every Young Adult Should Know | *For ages 16–23*

This is the book you just finished. It makes money feel manageable, hopeful, and not intimidating. Small, consistent choices made early can create freedom, options, and peace of mind over time. Getting free is the goal, not getting rich.

Start Smart Life Basics — Book 2

The Skills That Make Every Smart Decision Possible | *For ages 16–23*

Before you can make smart decisions about money or anything else, you need to understand how you make decisions and who you're making them for. This book builds the foundation: values, goals, time management, relationships, personal responsibility, and the self-awareness that ties it all together. It's not about having the right answers. It's about becoming the kind of person who knows how to find them.

Start Smart Quick Start Guide — Book 3

10 Money Principles Every Adult Should Know | *For adults 24+*

If no one taught you about money when you were starting out, this book meets you where you are, without judgment. The same 10 principles are applied to the realities of adult life. It's never too late to start smart.

Plan Now, Smile Later — Book 4

An Educator's Blueprint for Financial Success | *For adults ready to go deeper*

This is Kay's flagship work, a comprehensive guide to money and life planning built around the CAM framework, the Microscope/Telescope model, and the Ferris wheel of life balance. It helps you understand where you are, clarify where you want to go, and build a simple, sustainable plan to get there.